KNOW THY MAN

KNOW THY MAN

LEARN WHAT YOUR MAN IS THINKING
SECRETS MEN DO NOT WANT YOU TO KNOW

MANUEL V. JOHNSON

KNOW THY MAN

Published by: Manuel Johnson | Ask Dr Linq, LLC.

Ask Dr. Linq Book Collection

ISBN: 978-0-9861430-6-9
Library of Congress Control Number: 2024916726

Printed in United States of America
First Edition: October 2024

www.AskDrLinq.com

For permissions requests, contact:
AskDrLinqInfo@gmail.com

The information provided in this book, "KNOW THY MAN," is for general informational and educational purposes only. The content is based on the author's research, experiences, and opinions, and is not intended to be a substitute for professional medical advice, diagnosis, or treatment.

Readers should not disregard or delay seeking medical advice because of any information contained in this book. Always seek the guidance of your physician or other qualified health professionals with any questions you may have regarding your health or a medical condition. The author and publisher of "KNOW THY MAN" are not responsible for any adverse effects or consequences resulting from the use of any suggestions, products, or procedures described in this book.

By reading this book, you acknowledge and agree that you are solely responsible for your health and wellbeing, and that the author and publisher cannot be held liable for any loss or damage resulting from your reliance on the information presented herein

TABLE OF CONTENTS

THE GENESIS

Welcome to a heartfelt journey through the complexities of relationships. This book is a sanctuary of insights, born from countless conversations and experiences. Some of you will find closure from past heartaches, others will uncover new hopes for future connections, and many will discover practical wisdom to transform your current relationships. Just as art speaks to different souls in different ways, so too will these pages resonate uniquely with each of you.

For those who know my platform, you understand that my mission has always been to bring clarity and compassion to women seeking to understand the minds of men. This book continues that mission with even greater depth. Before we begin, I want to emphasize that majority of what you will read here is my personal philosophy, shaped by my own experiences and enriched by my interactions with thousands of women through emails and phone calls. I have also engaged deeply with men from all walks of life — whether married, single, abstinent, promiscuous, religious, non-believing, corporate, or those on the edge of society.

In these diverse stories, I have found a common thread, an unspoken understanding among men that women often don't see. While I don't hold a formal degree in this field, my real-world encounters and the authentic voices of those living these experiences offer a wisdom that is as profound as academic study…respectfully.

I genuinely hope this publication becomes a staple in the pages of your book of life, connecting thoughts you were never able to connect before.

May it help you heal, inspire you to share its insights with friends, and together, may we all do our part on this planet. Thank you from the bottom of my heart for taking this journey with me.

Overview

In this book, each chapter is titled "THE BOOK OF (insert name)" rather than using a traditional chapter number. This approach is designed to cultivate a deeper, more personal connection. To facilitate easy reference and note-taking, each subheading and paragraph is numbered.

For example, if you find something significant in The Book of Jasmine, section 3, paragraph 7, you can simply refer to it as **JASMINE 3:7**. This system not only makes sharing easier but also helps you remember and locate specific points you enjoyed effortlessly.

Each Book starts with a brief story to provide context and help you connect with the scenario. Following the story, you'll dive into the informative part of the Book.

So, buckle up—it's going to be a long ride.

KNOW THY MAN

THE BOOK OF

JASMINE

WHERE HAS HE GONE

I n the comfort of her bed, phone in hand, Jasmine contemplates whether the guy she gave her number to is genuinely interested. In those initial weeks, he epitomized the perfect gentleman—regular calls, swift responses to texts, and thoughtfully planned dates. Now, with her head against a plush pillow and limbs intertwined in her sheets, she eagerly awaits his response.

Reflecting on the cherished moments they've shared, Jasmine ponders the potential she once saw in him, now reduced to a distant memory. "*Am I overreacting?*" she questions herself. Striving to rationalize his recent behavior, she contemplates the possibility that his demanding work schedule might be to blame. As the sunsets and darkness blankets the sky, worry begins to gnaw at her. "*Maybe I moved too fast. Was it just a forgetful night for him?*" she wonders, a drop of regret coloring her thoughts.

After a couple of days, he finally decides to text her back. A simple *"Hello stranger"* appears on her screen. With an internal smile but a facial expression that hints at disbelief, she ponders on Kayden's return. It's not the first time he's gone off the grid for days. All Jasmine desires now is an understanding of why these sporadic disappearing acts have become a consistent pattern in their seemingly promising connection.

₁ **THE BEGINNING**

₁ I urge women to consistently seek their future husband when getting to know a guy. In essence, ensure that the man you are granting this special opportunity, possesses the qualities you desire in a *lifelong partner,* even if marriage isn't on your immediate horizon. Why? Simple, in the beginning, people typically experience the ***Infatuation Stage***. During this phase, women may find themselves blinded by many of his faults. You won't always notice them because excitement surrounds the fresh start of the relationship.

₂ Additionally, during this phase, you may find that you're striving to present yourself as the *"right woman"* for him. So, while focusing on making sure he likes you, you might overlook what he is revealing. His looks, job, and his material belongings are heightened during this *Infatuation Stage.* Those things are important but shouldn't overshadow his <u>character</u> and <u>personal mindset</u>. In the initial weeks, you may not prioritize his husband-like qualities, either because you aren't seeking a husband or simply want to enjoy the present without thinking too far ahead.

₃ However, I can assure you this will be crucial. If and when you develop strong feelings for this man, and his life achievements, looks, and belongings become routine, all that remains is his <u>character</u>. If he currently has a drinking problem, ask yourself if you want a husband with an alcohol addiction. May sound extreme, but always remember that most tragic downfalls start with one small, misguided decision.

4 If he prioritizes time with his male friends as much or more than with you, consider if this is something you can handle if it persists in marriage.

5 Let's be clear; I'm not saying one can't change their ways, but I'm not a fan of *hoping*, *wishing*, or *convincing* someone to change. I believe in addressing it early on before reaching a point where you're praying for change because you've fallen in love with someone incompatible with the future you envision. So always examine the man you are simply dating, one day your heart may become attached.

2 THE GREATEST TRICK

1 In navigating relationships, men often employ a subtle tactic—what I call **The Greatest Trick**—*especially when faced with women seeking something serious*. Many times, men may not even realize they're doing it.

2 Women often hesitate to ask for clarification on their relationship status, fearing it might scare the man away. This

dynamic sets the stage for a common scenario where a woman *hopes* a relationship will progress to the next level without clearly communicating her intentions from the start.

₃ The trick involves making a woman feel loved while simultaneously creating uncertainty about commitment. In other words, *show her you love her, but tell her you don't.* It may sound counterintuitive, but it's a powerful dynamic that makes it challenging for women to break away from men who have clearly stated they're not interested in a serious relationship. The initial excitement or *infatuation stage* in a relationship can blind women to the fact that their partner may not be as invested in a long-term relationship.

₄ Have you ever wondered why relationships that start off great often take a downward turn over time? This can possibly be a shift from the initial *Make her love me* phase to the complacency of *I know she loves me; I don't have to try anymore* phase. This shift can lead women to settle for less, accepting a mindset of *"He doesn't want a relationship, so I'll take what I can get,"* often this "what I can get" is limited to casual sex and laughter.

₅ I want to caution women considering a *"friends with benefits"* or *"no strings attached"* arrangement to carefully evaluate whether they can truly handle it, as the man likely can. While some men may catch deep feelings, most can manage the casual nature of such an arrangement.

6 Be prepared for the worst but expect the best. It's crucial *not* to enter these situations with expectations of failure; instead, approach them with thoughtful consideration.

7 If you find yourself dealing with a guy who has shown disinterest in a relationship, and you're contemplating waiting for him to *be ready*, that's your decision. However, if you're tired of hearing excuses for his lack of commitment, consider making a change in a different direction, even if his actions suggest he wants a committed relationship. That's the trick. *Treat* him like a <u>friend</u> if he verbally claims to want <u>friendship</u>—no physical involvement, just conversation—or even more powerfully, reclaim control of your life and move on.

8 Effective communication is important in any relationship, especially when it comes to serious matters. When getting to know someone, make your intentions clear. Find out what qualities he envisions in a future partner, and ensure you share those traits. However, it's important not to invest more than he has demonstrated. Balance is the key to a healthy dynamic.

9 I recall a woman named Megan who playfully asked her guy she *wasn't* in a relationship with if he was cheating

on her. His response to her was one of defense, indicating some level of commitment to only her, even if he might have been seeing other women. This shift in behavior demonstrated that he acknowledged her *expectation of exclusivity*. This isn't about forcing commitment on a man, but instead establishing a **relationship-or-nothing** policy. If he says, "*I'm not your man*," you'll know where you both stand—he's just a friend. Don't shy away from asking a man the tough questions. Buried in the tough questions is where you'll find the jewels of truth.

10 If Megan had received a different response, like him admitting to seeing other women, she would have had to decide whether she wanted to continue to share intimate connections with someone who's not exclusively dating her. That can lead to a deeper topic we'll explore further in the *Watering the Seed* section of this book.

11 Consider a scenario where a man envisions marrying you; constantly discussing a future together. If you were to suggest being *friends with benefits*, he likely wouldn't be okay with it. But a man uninterested in a future with you will happily step into that *F.W.B.* role. Sometimes, you have to throw out the bait to see which fish will bite.

₃ NEGATIVITY IS QUEEN

₁ There are two indicators of communication used to gauge his intentions: one is his actions, and the other is his words. They should both show the same thing – full interest in you.

₂ If his words were, "*I want to impregnate you tonight,*" his actions **shouldn't** indicate a lack of interest in having sex with you; instead, his actions would reflect an attempt to get you into bed tonight.

₃ If in your eyes, his *actions* suggest a desire for a relationship, his *words* should untimely convey, "*I want a relationship.*" If he's stating he **doesn't** want a relationship but engaging in relationship-like behavior, pay attention to the negative of the two indicators.

₄ It's in a guy's best interest to treat you special when you're not his official girlfriend. Why? Because he knows you have the option of talking to many other men. Being that he says he doesn't want to settle down just yet, he has to figure out a way to continue getting you to give yourself to him – or, as we say, "*Keep You on The Team.*"

₅ So, this may explain why his *words* might convey not wanting a relationship while his *actions* seem to suggest otherwise. It's meant to confuse you; most women seem to want to believe what they see over what they hear. Since actions are supposed to speak louder than words, guys use this ideology to their advantage.

₆ Now you may be asking, "*Why does he want me to continue dealing with him, even though he doesn't want me to be his lady?*" There could be several reasons, but the most basic and common reason is simply *sex*. For most men, sex doesn't come easy, even for those perceived to have *all the women*. He has a select type of woman he prefers, and most of those women "All over him" aren't her. Besides, for some men, you can never have too many women if you know how to juggle them right. But back to the point, pay close attention to the <u>negative</u> of the two indicators.

₇ In theory, when a man is not your man, if he has sex with other women, you shouldn't stress yourself because he is a *free* man and not obligated to be faithful to you. It may sound weird, but the purpose of commitment is to be committed to *one* woman. If he has not committed to you, how can he be held accountable? If you two are dating and he tells you that you are the only one he's sleeping with, he can then be held accountable. So, make sure you ask him directly. If he lies, you have every right to be upset without question.

- **When his actions are an A+ but his words are a D-, listen to his <u>words</u>.**
- **When his words are an A+ and his actions are a D-, listen to his <u>actions</u>.**

8 In other words, his words and actions must be aligned for you to continue dealing with him. This is how you avoid accepting mixed signals, as women often do.

IN COMMITMENT, <u>ACTIONS</u> RULE

9 When it comes to your man, he has a responsibility of commitment to you. So, you must hold him accountable for any negative action he may take. His words mean a tad bit less because if he says, "I love you," do his actions show that he loves you? That's what matters at that point – action. You must feel it more than you hear it.

10 If he says, "*I don't love you anymore*," examine his emotion behind this statement. Is it from a place of temporary anger like an argument, or a place of gloom like a cry to be alone in sorrow? It may be a temporary feeling due to his emotional state. In this scenario, his words may not represent his ultimate true feeling, especially if his actions continue to show that he does love you. But don't ignore those negative words altogether. Those particular words indicate that you should *begin* to pay closer attention to his actions.

₁₁ Negative actions that you may have let slide before must now be examined with a magnifying glass after negative words are said. Those negative words aren't what rule; his actions are. But enough of those negative words can at times show you more than any one action can. Their impact, when accumulated, can hurt or heal just as much over time.

₁₂ So, when you're committed, remember that commitment is the call to *action*. In theory, it goes, *"You say the right words to get the girl, and once you get her, you show her why you wanted her."* In commitment, action rules because commitment is an oath, so to speak – it's a promise.

WHEN DATING, <u>WORDS</u> RULE

₁₃ When you two are just dating, there is no promise, no oath, just an agreement to see each other again next Thursday. But commitment is like accepting a President. He goes on a voting campaign telling you what he will do once in office; you listen to his words. Once you vote him in, his words mean a tad bit less, and now his actions mean a whole lot more. That's commitment.

₁₄ But regardless of which indicator and in what relationship status you find yourself faced with, if they don't align, you must decline.

₄ **WHY DID HE CHANGE**

₁ After some time, he might start acting distant. This could be because he got what he wanted from you and is now done with the situation. Another reason could be that he misunderstood his own feelings. Maybe he thought he was really into you, but once things got physical a few times, those feelings faded. It happens a lot where guys mix up their desire for a woman with actual love. Sometimes, women think a guy just lied about his feelings and only wanted the physical part. While that can be true, there's also a chance he genuinely believed he wanted more, and it changed along the way.

₂ Additionally, his changes might be because he saw something in you he didn't like and didn't want to deal with anymore. Let's hope that's not the case. But even if it is, it doesn't mean there's something wrong with you or him. It just means you two weren't the right match from the start. It means his first impression of you wasn't accurate.

₃ People go through changes for many reasons, as we can see. The key is to understand where you stand through it all – knowing what you are to each other and what's expected. Your role is to hold him to the standards and expectations set in the beginning. If he sticks to them, you've done your part. If he starts breaking them, then you need to take action.

4 Every new relationship involves risk, no guarantees, and uncertain outcomes. So, approach each new situation with caution. Hold him responsible for his actions and let him know if he's crossing your boundaries. Don't be afraid to demand respect early on. He, as a man, will either back off or respect your wishes, honoring you for the person you've shown him. He should have his own standards too. A man who lets you do anything to him is an open target for most women.

5 Remember, a guy will treat you based on what you allow. It's never smart to trade your self-respect for your feelings. In other words, no matter how much you want it to work, stand firm on your principles. That's what we've got in the end.

5 WASTE OF OUR TIME

1 Have you ever been in a situation where a guy persistently asks for your phone number, especially on social media? You finally share it, only for him to vanish after a few *"good morning"* texts, leaving you questioning the purpose of his pursuit.

2 It's crucial to recognize that many men are wired to chase – it's tied to their sense of masculinity. The pursuit

keeps them engaged, even if they don't envision a future with you. The success of the chase fulfills their inherent need until the next pursuit arises.

3 Furthermore, the modern man is evolving alongside the modern woman. Having encountered women who've used him for dates of free food, drinks, and entertainment, he now seeks equal effort. He wants assurance that the woman he is investing in is as invested in him as he is in her. If he perceives a lack of effort on her part, he withdraws. The modern man isn't interested in convincing you he is worthy of being with you without confirmation of lasting interest beyond just sharing a phone number on your behalf. So if he's seeing any lack of effort, he retreats.

4 Moreover, men who vanish after getting your number might have become jaded with the chase. After chasing countless women and gathering numerous personal contacts, the pursuit begins to feel like an endless quest for fleeting happiness. So, in the midst of the chase, he simply gives up.

5 At day's end, our well-being depends on the mindful choices that shape our lives with positivity. It becomes vital to cherish relationships and interactions that uplift our mental and emotional state. By gently distancing ourselves from individuals or situations that clash with our positive energy,

we cultivate a space that nurtures our overall well-being. This art of selective engagement is a cornerstone of self-care, reminding us that safeguarding our mental and emotional health is a paramount priority in our daily journey.

Read Jasmine's story again, what do you think she should do?

"... A GUY WILL TREAT YOU BASED ON WHAT YOU ALLOW. IT'S NEVER SMART TO TRADE YOUR SELF-RESPECT FOR YOUR FEELINGS."

- MANUEL V. JOHNSON | JASMINE 4:5

THE BOOK OF

LAUREN

I THINK HE'S THE ONE, BUT AM I THE ONLY ONE

L auren, with a heart of excitement, believed that the turbulent times were finally behind them. The initial phase of their relationship had been rocky, as many are. There were moments when doubt lingered, questioning Caleb's intentions, suspecting him of seeking only physical intimacy. Yet, in the dance of time, Caleb proved himself to be more. He patiently waited for three months before their relationship blossomed in a physical one, eventually showing Lauren an erotic side of him she hadn't anticipated. Fast forward five months, and Lauren found herself immersed in Caleb's world. She had met his mother, his child, and a circle of his closest friends. Expressions of love flowed freely between them, weaving a web of shared dreams and aspirations. Though residing in separate homes for now, discussions about eventually moving in together had filled their nights. Lying in bed after a delightful evening, they playfully explored the hypothetical details of a future wedding, discussing colors, bridesmaids, and groomsmen. The trajectory of their relationship seemed positively set.

However, nestled in the cocoon of contentment, a seed of doubt sprouted in Lauren's mind. A fleeting curiosity led her to explore Caleb's social media presence. As she delved deeper, she realized that, to the external world, he might appear to be a solitary figure living a seemingly single life. The initial warmth began to cool as doubt slithered through her thoughts like a snake in a dry field of grass. An unsettling realization tightened her stomach - the possibility that Caleb might be keeping their relationship a secret from the world. Despite the undeniable bond they shared in private, the nagging question lingered: *"Am I a secret?"* The uncer-

tainty cast a shadow over the once bright landscape of their

relationship, leaving Lauren in a contemplative state, grap-

pling with the duality that now clouded her perception of

their love.

₁ **WATERING THE SEED**

₁ **Watering the Seed** is typically used when a man is faced with a woman who wishes to hold off on sexual intimacy. The concept originates from planting a seed in soil, watering it, and allowing it to grow into a tree with ripe fruit. While one tree grows, you consume fruit from others you've previously planted. The idea is not to cease watering the tree just because you have others; in fact, you lavish more attention on the new tree until it's ready to be plucked. Similar to a pimp and his prostitutes, where more time is spent with the new girl to establish a connection.

₂ He doesn't stop enjoying other trees' fruit while waiting for the new one to grow; he has reserves. Applying this to your situation, you are the seed, the soil is friendship, and his water is expressed through thoughtful texts and calls, as well as his gestures like bringing you food without being told. The plucking of fruit, symbolizing the act of sex, occurs when you are ready. The key point is that a man will wait for sex if he can still have sex with other women. He might water multiple seeds, and the one that sprouts the fastest gets harvested first. This behavior is common among men with less active schedules and few responsibilities.

₃ Waiting for three months may not necessarily mean he's *abstinent* during that time. It's crucial to recognize that the idea of abstaining might be more <u>yours</u> than his. Does it mean you shouldn't make a guy wait? Not necessarily.

₄ There are guys who will leave you alone after realizing you two aren't getting anywhere sexually, and this is good because it weeds out the weak. His text messages will slow down, and his concern for you will begin to fade. Guys in their 20s tend to wait a little longer because they usually have more *women* on their *team* or more *trees* in their *forest*. They have fewer issues with waiting, even though their sexual energy is higher than that of older men.

₅ Guys in their 30s and above are less likely to play along with your waiting game for as long. They have little patience because the game of sleeping with multiple women is routine for them; they're ready to get straight to the point. Time is limited, and they don't have the luxury to sit on the phone and talk about your day when they really don't care. They usually have more responsibilities, so adding another person to their daily routine can become too much, especially if there is no sexual reward for it. They eventually expose themselves by saying things like, *"I'm too grown to be playing around."* Not realizing that they're the ones playing. Unless he was clear in the beginning that this was a *"Sex-uation"* (sexual situation), then he's not playing; he's just ready for the sex part you agreed to.

₆ There's no way of avoiding the watering process; just be mindful of its existence and act accordingly. All you can do is steer the conversation to an informative one, a conversation about the mind, not physical appearance. Try to learn something new about each other every day, instead of merely talking about each other's day. Talk on the phone *more* and text *less*.

₇ In today's world, guys often want to *digitally* text you to see how you're physically doing, just so they can come over later and *physically* do you. See how it works? Spark conversations about who you are mentally; talk about your mental status. Speak to topics that require deep thought. See where his mental state is and where he wants it to be. So maybe later, you two can *mentally* stimulate each other before you physically stimulate one another. But all of this should be over the phone or in person, not through text messages. He has to work his lips and work his mind in order to converse with you. There won't be any 'digital texting while physically hugging on another women' going on.

₈ Remember, in the beginning stages of the connection between you and he, just because he is waiting for sex, doesn't mean he is *waiting* for sex. Does he have to be faithful to someone he has not committed to? Not necessarily. But if you want him to be committed, ask him to answer a simple question that may steer the relationship, *"Are you having sex with anyone?"* If he says, *"No,"* and you find out he is, he's a liar and you can do with that information as you will. If he says, *"Yes,"* you must decide if you want to share this man with another woman. What you are establishing is a conversational base where who he sleeps with is now a topic of concern. He now realizes the fruit of his answer will determine your perception of him and your perception of him will determine if he gets what he wants from you or not. Forcing him to either, 1) run his game with caution, 2) tell the truth or 3) leave because things just got serious.

₉ In my opinion, single men should experience turning down beautiful women sexually before entering a relationship. He needs a few *"No's"* under his belt. Relying solely on a relationship as a reason not to cheat may falter under moments of selfishness or anger. While this may be uncommon, it doesn't mean it's illogical. How can he know he possesses the discipline to deny his urges if he's never faced them and prevailed? Mastering the art of restraints is essential for a devoted relationship.

₁₀ Having the strength to say "**NO**" comes easier if the power to resist is already within. If a guy has never turned down sex or told a pretty woman, *"No thank you"* when an opportunity for sex emerges, he may find it difficult to say *"no"* for the <u>first time</u>, even if he is in a relationship. Especially if he hasn't come to grips with the idea beforehand. It seems that many women are offered sex from men, more often than men are offered from women. So most women have had <u>practice</u> saying, *"No"* regularly; most men have not.

2 **THE TROPHY EFFECT**

1 I've met many women who have been brainwashed with the idea that meeting a guy's parents automatically means he's on the road to commitment. Unfortunately, this is not always true. Some guys will simply introduce a girl to his mother because she's beautiful. If she is at the location you both are going to, he may ask you to meet her as well. One thing meeting his mother probably does prove is, you're pretty enough for him to show you off. It doesn't mean he has some future plans with you; it just lets you know he views your physical features as worthy to be seen next to him.

2 Meeting someone's child may seem like a big deal, but for some people, its commonplace. They've met their moms' boyfriends regularly and grew up just fine, so what's the problem? You see, that being of importance varies per individual.

3 This also applies to meeting his friends. Some guys don't introduce the woman they are dating to their friends

for many reasons, including trust issues amongst each other. But some do because it's normally what they do with all their new women, especially a woman with a beautiful face and an attractive physique. He can't wait to show her off, like a trophy of his accomplishments. You may be one of the few "trophies" he has brought around his close family and friends; that's a plus. Should it be viewed as a good thing to meet people who are close to him? Yes, but should you hold that as some type of accomplishment? Not necessarily. Who you met *outside* of him, doesn't show you who's *inside* of him. That's what matters most. So while scratching the surface is a start, remember that you probably could have found his mom and friends on his social media page. So what exactly has he really **shown** you that no one else has seen?

3 THE SOCIAL EXCHANGE

i Many guys in relationships have used numerous excuses for not wanting to share pictures of their women on their social media pages. But none more than the, *"I'm just a private person, and I don't want anyone in my business like that"* reason. Guys will go as far as to stop taking pictures of themselves once in a relationship just to keep this statement of privacy true. Then there are those who continue to post themselves and share their personal lives, all while saying, *"I want privacy online."* If he truly wants privacy, should he not delete his social media platforms? I mean, isn't that the ultimate privacy?

2 If he can show off his new shoes, he shouldn't have an issue doing the same with you. Not that you're an object, but because you bring him joy. Online, we share things we're proud of, things we love, like, laugh, and cry about. Don't you fit at least one of those categories?

3 In most cases, he simply doesn't want to upset the other female friends he's seeing. Even if he isn't seeing them right now, he doesn't want to shut the door on a chance to sleep with them. That is key. He will tell you, *"I'm not seeing any of those women,"* while that may be true, it doesn't mean he isn't leaving the potential open to do just that. So essentially you being on his page may mess that up.

4 Now, we all know that there are women who don't even care if a man is in a relationship or not. Hell, some women are more attracted to men who are. But a guy normally doesn't want to take the chance of messing his *perceived availability* up, so his natural reaction is to hide you to appear obtainable still.

5 Let's say he knows that his side chick is currently okay with him having a girlfriend now, if she continues to regularly witness you and him in pictures, she may get

frustrated, tired of it and simply move on from him. He doesn't want it to get to that point, so he limits your public showing. Plus, if he's telling them/her all the bad things about you and all the reasons why he wants to leave you, it's going to seem odd to her to see you in a picture with him smiling like you two just got married. In order to keep his lies alive to these women, he has to play the part, and that may be to keep you hidden as if there are problems between him and you.

6 Women often have no problem sleeping with men who claim they are having girlfriend problems and are soon to be single. The thought of taking a woman's man can fuel her egotistical selfishness.

7 So where does all this leave you? Understand that he can't hide you from anyone. What exactly could the reason be….so that other people can't see you. But we have to ask, from whom? Well, if you've met his family or friends, it's not them, especially if he's excited about showing you off to them. So why is he so distant with you on his social media platforms? It's possible that he doesn't want men to know who his woman is because he's afraid they may try to inbox you and try to sleep with you as revenge for something he's done, depending on his lifestyle or previous lifestyle. But that raises the question of his trust for you. No matter how many guys may talk to you, if he's been a stand-

up man and he feels you're a stand-up woman, there should-n't be worries of you stepping out. If that worries him, I'm sure *Girls Night Out* would drive him to a coma.

₈ I'd say it's more than likely because his other women/po-tential women are on his page, and he doesn't want to ruffle any feathers. His concern for these other women's feelings over yours speaks to his selfishness. A relationship is not solely about what makes one person happy; it's about mu-tual respect, care, and making sure both partners feel valued and secure. If he values their *hurt* above yours, the relation-ship is doomed until he changes that.

₉ Besides the privacy excuse I used earlier in this section, here are some other excuses he may use:

- "My child's mother is crazy, and I don't want her to put me on child support."
- "I do music, and it will mess up my image for the fans. I have to keep them fantasizing."
- "My family is nosy and always has something nega-tive to say, and I don't want to hear it."
- "I'm just not a picture kind of guy."
- "It's just social media; it's not real life anyway."
- "What does it matter what they think, as long as we love each other in real life?"
- "In my line of work, a lot of my clients are women. They may stop doing business with me if they find out I have someone."

Some of these are situational excuses. If he doesn't have a kid, the first one obviously will not apply. But nonetheless, they are regularly used.

10 Now, the bottom line is if he really loves or likes you, and you are an official couple, he should not have a problem showing you to the world. You want someone to be proud to be with you. Not someone who is controlled by outside forces, which in turn forces you to play second hand to those who control him.

11 Remember, while showing you on his social media page doesn't mean *marriage*; it can show claim of the relationship. A relationship doesn't start and end with social media, but let's not act like there is a robot running his social media page; it is him, his thoughts, and his words. So it holds *some* weight in his life. If social media means nothing to him, he shouldn't mind you taking control of his page then, *right?*

12 If social media holds little significance in *your* life, then this matter may not resonate with you. I recognize the concept of keeping your significant other private, but I also acknowledge it as a manifestation of insecurity. It implies a lack of confidence in the strength of your relationship, leading you to go to great lengths to shield your partner from tempting attention. I understand the sentiment though.

However, I propose that genuine relationships undergo trials and yet invariably discover paths to endure and thrive. And that is how you build confidence to have a long-lasting partnership.

Read Lauren's story again, what do you think she should do?

"...SINGLE MEN SHOULD EXPERIENCE TURNING DOWN BEAUTIFUL WOMEN S**UALLY BEFORE ENTERING A RELATIONSHIP. HE NEEDS A FEW *"NO'S"* UNDER HIS BELT.

- MANUEL V. JOHNSON | LAUREN 1:9

THE BOOK OF

ANGIE

WHY CAN'T I LET HIM GO

A ngie and Mike have been dating for five years now. They have a beautiful two-year-old child together. But it hasn't been the loving ride they had expected.

In the very beginning of their relationship, Angie questioned Mike about having kids. He denied having any children. A year into their relationship she receives an inbox online. It was from a woman she had never met before. The woman on the other end informed Angie that she too had been dating the same guy and in fact she was pregnant by Mike. Angie was highly upset and couldn't believe what she was reading. She asked Mike about the woman and his alleged child; she even let him see the message. His response ultimately was, *"She's lying."* Angie loved her man and as time went on, the situation dwindled away, and she forced herself to believe him.

Eleven months later when Angie was visiting her family out of town, she received a concerned phone call from Mike's mother who sounded bothered with something. She confessed that her son had another child from another woman and stressed that he wasn't in the child's life how she wanted him to be. His mother felt that Mike's lack of attention to this newfound child was due to Angie being around and she didn't approve of this secrecy. Angie didn't want to believe it, but she couldn't just sweep it under the rug this time. She came back home to address the issue face to face. After hours of, *"Why are you tripping?"* questions, he finally admitted that he had slept with someone else, but he claimed it was just once. He stressed that the baby was more than likely not his because it was a one-time situation. She wanted answers, so she encouraged him to take a DNA test. He did, the baby turned out to be his. Angie was upset but more importantly cut deep by the shattered glass of her trust. She later found out that this woman was in fact someone he knew from middle school.

Angie and Mike split and moved into separate apartments; she couldn't deal with the pain she felt every time she saw his face. Angie loved her man unconditionally. So, after months of slowly communicating with one another, they became a couple again. *"He has a baby, we have a baby,"* became her motto. She was very supportive of the situation even though she was somewhat hurt. She eventually developed a cordial relationship with the other child's mother as well.

They continued to stay in separate places and that concerned Angie, but they proceeded to see one another.

In time Angie also became pregnant with his child. She was excited and felt even more connected to the man she so deeply loved. But their separate living conditions continued to concern her regarding his faithfulness. She asked him if he was still sleeping with his other child's mother, and he assured her that he wasn't. She trusted him, but not enough to keep her from his phone. One day she went through it and found some alarming pictures and messages. Messages from a woman she has never seen. When questioned, Mike gave her the same rhetoric he normally does.

They split again but, in a few months, they were back as if nothing happened.

Some time passed and she found out he still was having sex with his child's mother as well. Mike wasn't a new man at all, he simply hasn't changed. At this point, Angie was tired of the cycle she seems to be trapped in. She just wants to get out and into a situation that is more productive to a positive life. But for some reason she can't seem to break away from his grasps. Even though she can see he is not what she needs, he continues to be the one she wants.

₁ STUCK IN PARADISE

₁ The reason you may feel that you can't leave him alone is because of *hope, faith, and belief.* You still feel there is a chance that you two can be as one. This is understandable since most relationships have good times as well. These good times are highlighted because they happen more frequently. A good massage while watching a movie can be a good night. When you have a hundred of those moments and just two to three negative experiences, it becomes difficult to end the relationship based on the odds of 3% negative and 97% positive, but that's **Quantity** talk.

₂ The counterpoint from **Quality** talk says, *"Sleeping with your sister is 1 bad time out of 99 good times, but that 1 bad time's <u>impact</u> is greater than 1,000 good times."*

₃ There's also a level of comfort with someone you've invested time in. Who wants to start over with someone else? But understand that this question is essentially part of the issue. Never view it as having to *start over with someone else.* Instead, view it as *improving your life with a fresh start*, emphasis on **your**. When you exit a relationship, it's not time to look outside yourself for another partner; it's an opportunity to look inside. When you step *outside* your house, you don't think about walking back into your house. You think about what you're about to do now that you're outside. The *opposite* of a breakup is being single, single meaning <u>one</u>, **you**. The *opposite* is not, *"Okay, who's next?"*

₄ Also, why you may feel stuck is because you probably haven't reached the point where you *need* it to be over, you merely *want* it to be over. You haven't become perturbed enough to override the deeply rooted love you still have for him. When you get to a point where your sanity needs to be freed, you'll find your willpower there.

₅ Sex. Sometimes when he's great in bed, or even worse, the best you've ever had, letting go can be challenging. It can also introduce a sense of fear. Fear that you won't be able to find someone who makes your body feel the way he does. Fear that you will live a life unsatisfied. Sex is one of the most focused moments two people share —with only being compared to meditation and prayer. Severing the bond that ignites your lust is no easy task. You triumph over this challenge by mastering the lustful energy within. Embrace abstinence and cleanse your desires to find freedom. That means no sex and no porn. So tuck that Rose away deep into your dresser drawer.

₆ Lastly, a reason you may feel that you can't leave him alone is because you want to be the woman that wins him. You may not see it like that, but we as humans have the competitive spirit rooted deep down inside of us. If he chooses you, it must mean you are the better woman. Even though the *"reward"* you'd be getting might not hold much value; it's a reward, nonetheless. *Winning him* boosts your ego and feeds your self-confidence, even if the prize is nothing more than a bag of shit.

₇ Consciously you may want to end it with him, but subconsciously you don't. What we have to do is create habits and a lifestyle that don't include him. That way your victory isn't *winning him*, your victory is now your *growth from him*.

1. You must replace thoughts of him with a goal in life. Something big you want to accomplish that will benefit your life and your child's life; preferably something positive that requires focus. Like a new dedication to working out with a diet plan, going back to school, or a new home business you wanted to get involved with. Any major goal of improvement will do. The idea is to remove your old love by building your new love and dispense your focus and time upon it. The love for your child will remain high as it did in the relationship; the same for your job. The only thing we'll be replacing is **him** for something that helps you grow.

2. You must view him as the enemy.
Not necessarily a *"bad person,"* but a virtual enemy that's trying to stop you from accomplishing the goal of leaving.

View him as someone who may love you, but is purposely trying to confuse and hurt you. He's not the happiness inside you; he's the roadblock on your way to finding the happiness inside you. If you want to leave him alone, you must see him as an evil spirit or a negative entity. This will make rejecting him much easier. You can use this with everyday things you want to remove from your life as well. I had a smoking habit I kicked a few years back. I did it by visualizing my urge to smoke as an evil entity trying to keep me as his slave to the cigar. Every time my craving kicked in, I laughed and said, *"Nope! You're not going to get me, Sir!"* Weird I know, but it worked. Once you can see the temptation as it formulates, you can label it, and now you have a face to fight. But when you don't have a face, you end up just fighting yourself.

3. You have to establish a new relationship with him - a relationship that only requires communication when it is concerning the child.

Oftentimes people create a median between themselves - someone who can communicate between both parties; a mother or relative. I suggest you two remain in communication but keep conversations short and on-topic. No need to reminisce and crack jokes. **Until** you two have clearly moved on mentally, then it's healthy to have an overly communicative relationship with your child's opposite parent. You two can get a lot accomplished *for* your child by having a short conversation *about* your child. Check each other's state of mind as a safety precaution for your child and keep it moving. I say this because often we confuse missing someone with wanting to be with someone. Excessive talks of the past and constantly bringing up the *good old times* can cause you to make decisions based on a yearning for an old life that doesn't exist anywhere else but in the memories of both of you. Positive excessive talks about the present can cause intrigue and strike curiosity of a potential future together. Stay clear of these conversations.

8 For the women reading this who may not have a child with the person they're trying to let go, I have your fourth suggestion here.

4. Since there is no kid involved, I'm assuming you want to remove them from your life fully. You will undoubtedly have to remove them from your social media pages.

It's perfectly okay to unfollow someone you want to get over. I even recommend blocking them if you find yourself visiting their page. You must delete their number and delete their text message thread. Delete all their photos out of your phone or simply put them on a USB drive so you still have them, if need be, but they can't be at your fingertips. We use our senses to interact with people, so if we can stop them from interacting with these senses, we can reduce the desire to be around them. All that will be left is our memories, and with time those will fade.

₉ As the old saying states, *"Where the attention goes, the energy flows."*

₂ DEALING WITH HIS BABY MAMA

₁ This topic in general has a wide range of perspectives, situational angles and circumstances.

- **Dealing with a baby mother that came <u>before</u> you is probably most common and most accepted by women in these dynamics.**

₂ Once you reach a certain age, you will notice that most men are already fathers. The average man has his first child at around 25 years of age. At this age range, you will be virtually forced to find someone with a child. The pool of childless men starts to get far and few as you approach the late 20s of men.

₃ You can learn a lot from a man by how he and his child's mother interact and his choice of words when speaking about her. Regardless of what he says, he decided to plant his seed inside this person. When a child is involved, I feel two adults should be able to be just that, adults. Communicate for the sake of the child and conduct themselves with respect and decorum. When a man and his child's mother aren't in a good space, it automatically puts you in a negative space with her as well. If he and she have zero communication, one has to wonder how this may affect the child. Is he okay with unhealthy co-parenting? I can understand how he and the mother having less communication might selfishly make you a little happy being that he's less likely seeing her still. But what does this say about how he may handle you? Understand that these actions may differ for you, but they may not. Does he have a *"Screw it"* attitude towards the situation, or does he want to address it for the betterment of his kid? These are the little things to watch.

4 Now, in this scenario where he and his child's mother are not speaking, you have no dealings with her as a result. But with an initial effort and outreach from him to her, you can position yourself as the median between them with his approval. Oftentimes the bridge between two individuals is burnt without repair, while putting the child in limbo. A father who would love to see his child and a mother who would love her child to be with his father sometimes are victims of their own egos. You being the sane mind in the situation with no animosity attached can come in and accept the role of a parent. This can mend their parent

friendship as well as put you in a place of control of the situation in some way.

5 But, there is absolutely nothing wrong with you simply letting them handle it themselves and playing the cards as they are. It's not your <u>job</u> to fix their friendship. But as a friend, girlfriend, and wife, it will help relieve the burden of the situation by helping him mend the communication gap between him and his child.

6 How do you handle the situation when their relationship becomes too friendly and too close? Like when he has a day where he's over there playing with his son and *"falls asleep"* on her couch so he can't answer the phone...yeah, those days.

7 Well, when you two are in a relationship, he must respect both parties, the same way you have to respect their communication. But in respecting both parties, he can't place the one he is no longer committed to over the one he is currently committed to. His and her relationship is no more; they are supposed to be free from one another's expectations. The only expectations that should be placed now are parental expectations. Being that their relationship has ended and yours has begun, he must make the transition. She isn't allowed to have the same access to him she once had and he needs to make that clear to her, you shouldn't have to. It's his place

to tell her she can't call him at 2am to talk about random things not concerning his child. She should have respect for you and his relationship, and he should demand that respect. At no point should she feel she has a greater place in his life—her child should, but not her. He's your man and her child's father. Her connection to him is the child; your connection to him is *him*. I'm talking serious relationships here, not if you and he are simply just dating.

8 Women often question whether or not a man is still sleeping with his child's mother. It happens often, but just as often it's a dead situation, and they no longer have sex. Most men don't sleep with their child's mother because the mother doesn't want to sleep with him. She's oftentimes moved on and no longer wants to be used, even though he still may try to and/or flirt with her.

9 The second reason he may not sleep with her would be because he knows she can't keep it a secret and would tell the world, in turn ending his current relationship with you. So he doesn't want to risk it even though the want for sex with her is there.

10 Many times when the mother hasn't moved on in her life and/or her relationship with your man didn't end well, she is upset at the perceived happiness of your relationship with him. It didn't work with her, and so by it seeming to work

with you, it appears that she is the bad puzzle piece. When in fact, some people just mesh better with others.

11 In order for her to feel back in control, back at the head and worth more to him, she tempts him with sex. And he, being comfortable with her and realizing that she has accepted his girlfriend/wife/you, it makes his decision to sleep with her fairly easy. She enjoys it because in her mind she feels, *"He may be with you, but deep down inside he still wants m*e." When in fact he just wanted sex, not her.

12 Speaking of good sex, occasionally she may just miss his sex and is not ready to let it go just yet. She may have zero feelings for **him** but may have all the *feels* for his extended piece below. And again, him realizing that his penis is that important to her boosts his ego and makes his decision to sleep with her very easy. It doesn't take much for us men sometimes. But sometimes sex with no perceived strings attached can be undeniable when facing a man who doesn't have discipline.

- **Dealing with a baby mother that came <u>during</u> your time with him is uncommon, but it happens more than it should.**

13 To many, it's regarded as one of the most disrespectful acts a man can commit to a woman he claims he loves. The very

simple answer is, "You don't deal with it," and I wouldn't judge any woman not wanting to. In fact, I'd more than likely support her decision.

14 But everyone's situation is different, and every woman's tolerance level is set at a different resistance point. When you've invested your life into someone, it's not easy to end it with them because it feels like you're ending your life. So I fully understand why some women stay and work through this type of scenario. I just simply do not *recommend* it.

15 For those who choose to work through this situation, you first must tackle his infidelity. His cheating is what led to this, and that cheating is what you are going to have to accept.

16 Then you have to accept the fact that more than likely he purposely had unprotected sex with this woman. Even if the condom popped (like he may have explained), there's still a *50/50* chance he noticed it before he ejaculated inside her and kept going. He ultimately put himself and you in harms way. If he's not committed to her, she is free to see who she wants. I'm sure she has exercised her options. As a result, she has whatever disease that guy may have, and he has what all the women he's slept with has. Now your man has it, and ultimately you have what they all have - hopefully nothing.

17 Along with accepting the infidelity and unprotected sex, you have to accept the level of disrespect and lack of precaution taken. It's not only having unprotected sex but to ejaculate inside her.

18 Lastly, you have to accept his child and deal with its mother. You may not want to deal with the mother directly, but she will now have to co-parent with your man, and his issues are your issues.

19 In dealing with this situation, there will be a lot of accepting and forgiving that will need to take place in order to move forward. If you can accept that, you two can start on your way to building your future together.

20 Once you've forgiven him, new ground rules must be laid down. Their communication must be limited. I understand that this is the mother of his child now, but these two have shown lack of respect for your relationship—more him than her. We aren't sure if she ever knew about you to begin with. If she didn't know, she's somewhat innocent. If she did know about you, what's stopping her from popping out baby number two with him?

21 I've seen couples in this predicament communicate through the women only. The girlfriend/wife and the child's mother build a relationship that's solely based around the

child. Not a friendship, but a partnership for the sake of the child. They divide the responsibility up between themselves.

22 The problem I have with this is that there is a lack of trust there. Trust with your man has been broken. Will you ever trust him around her? Will you trust him at all? It's very difficult to move forward when your new foundation doesn't have trust in it. So think long and hard before you decide to be with this man after his risky decision making. It may not be wise to raise a child with someone willing to risk it all for sex.

- **Dealing with a baby mother that came during your <u>breakup</u> and reconnection from each other is probably the least common, but it's a reality some women face**.

23 It's hard to accept the idea of another woman with your man. But when he isn't your man anymore, does it make it any easier to think about? I guess that would depend on how much you still cared for him. Oftentimes we tell ourselves that we can handle losing someone or that we couldn't care less if we see them with other people. But sometimes we don't know how we'll react until it happens.

24 When a couple separates, they are no longer tied to their commitment. So frankly, they can do what they want.

Normally they begin to miss one another and all the problems that were never fixed are forgotten. Until they reunite, then those problems will show their ugly face again. These problems will never go away until you two address them and come to some agreement or agree to simply stay apart. This is why a break can be useless in some cases. The problem wasn't you both being together; the problem was the disagreement that led to you both *not* being together. So by merely separating or taking some time for yourself, you're putting a Band-Aid over a bullet wound and oftentimes prolonging the inevitable.

25 Also, a break gives a man the opportunity to experience the things that were dwelling inside of him the entire time. Whether that is more time with his friends, or more time with other women. A break can show you who he truly is inside.

26 A dog in a small cage will lie down a lot more than a dog free to roam and explore. The dog is always the dog; but it's more about the limitations that are set upon him. There's a difference in a man that wants to sleep with only you versus a man that wants to sleep with other women, but doesn't solely because he does not want to get caught cheating. One has no urge and the other is fighting a war inside; a war he may lose from time to time.

27 It's worth some concern if your breakup wasn't for a long-extended period and he still managed to impregnate another woman. Unprotected sex with someone from his past is much more common due to the familiarity of the individual, opposed to the idea of unprotected sex with someone new.

28 So if this new baby mother is someone from his past, we now must question if he was sleeping with her during the relationship and not just during this break. If this new baby mother is a new woman in his life, we now must question his decision-making skills, especially if this break wasn't long. If the break wasn't long, when did he *actually* meet her? A child should be made with future plans of building a family, not just because it feels good in the moment. If you didn't want a child yesterday at work, you shouldn't want one while you're naked in bed. His life choices need to be examined.

29 Also, as a side note, keep track of when the child is born and make sure it lines up with the time you two were apart. You two were on a two-month break, and a month later this woman is six months pregnant—something isn't right.

30 In dealing with this situation, just as in the previous ones, a new level of trust must be built, and a great

acceptance must be obtained. Also, an understanding that this child is now *your* child as well and all major family decisions should include this kid. You can't accept him back without accepting what he has brought back with him. That's easier said than done, I know. Coming back from a relationship already indicates that things were rocky. Only to have him make things more complicated with a child.

31 As previously stated, he should understand where you and she stand in relation to him—you being connected directly to him and her being connected only through the child. It should show in his actions. Sometimes it's too much for men to balance, but he needs to adapt to this new situation for the sake of his own well-being. He has his woman back; he has a new child, and the child's mother. Along with the day-to-day problems life brings; it can be a bit much. It may be wise to prolong your reuniting or dismiss the idea altogether. But with accepting his new state, a new level of support will be asked of you as his woman. This can't be looked at as a *"That's your problem, handle it."* situation. Either you embrace it and rebuild with him or don't and go your separate ways.

32 Remember, this child was created during a time of separation; it's not what broke you two up, it's the result of what happened while on break. Don't blame the child indirectly.

33 If you and he already have children together, there's no reason why this new child should interfere with the others. It will be his duty to do more and increase his support to provide for both parties.

34 For many women, this is a deal breaker, and understandably so. You agreed to one thing and received another. Now, you have this new woman attached to your man, which can add new worry to an already fragile situation. So, it's very common that a woman wouldn't want to take on the task of playing stepmother and would instead let the *break* remain, well…. *broken.*

Read Angie's story again, what do you think she should do?

"HE'S NOT THE HAPPINESS INSIDE YOU; HE'S THE ROADBLOCK ON YOUR WAY TO FINDING THE HAPPINESS INSIDE YOU."

- MANUEL V. JOHNSON | ANGIE 1:7.2

THE BOOK OF

NINA

WILL WE EVER PROGRESS & GET MARRIED

Nina sat on the edge of her bed in the suffocating darkness, absentmindedly twirling her Promise Ring around her finger. Her mind was a whirlwind of thoughts and doubts, wondering where her relationship with Darin was headed. After eight long years together, what once felt like an exciting journey now seemed to have come to a standstill. She had always dreamed of marrying the man she loved and having children. While part of that dream had come true—she had a child from a previous relationship. She found love with

Darin, but the finishing part of her dream seemed out of reach. Nina had made her desire to be married clear countless times, but Darin never seemed to share her enthusiasm. The Promise Ring he gave her many years ago, now worn and dull, was a symbol from a time of pain and forgiveness. Looking back, she realized that the ring had been a *Get out of the Doghouse-FREE* card for Darin; a way for him to buy more time, a tool to delay the inevitable conversations about marriage.

Three years after accepting his *"promise"* ring, Nina stopped bringing up the topic of marriage altogether. She had decided to *go with the flow*, suppressing her own desires in the hope that things would eventually change. But deep down, the question never left her mind. *"Will we ever progress?"* a pang of sadness echoing through her heart.

Every night, as she lay next to Darin in the dark, she couldn't help but feel a growing sense of unease. The silence between them felt heavier with each passing day. She remembered the joy and excitement of their early days together, the plans they made, and the dreams they shared.

Now, those dreams felt like distant memories, overshadowed by the stagnation that had crept into their lives. Nina glanced at the clock, its neon glow piercing the darkness, marking the late hour. She sighed deeply, feeling the weight of the years pressing down on her. Her child, now older and more perceptive, had started to ask questions too. *"When are you and Darin getting married?"* they'd ask innocently, eyes full of curiosity. Nina never had a good answer.

She stood up slowly, walking to the window and looking out into the quiet night. The world outside seemed so still, yet within her, a storm raged on. She wondered if Darin even realized how much this unresolved issue hurt her. Did he see the sadness in her eyes? Did he feel the distance growing between them?

The Promise Ring, once a symbol of hope and commitment, now felt like a shackle. It reminded her of unfulfilled promises and lingering doubts. She twisted it around her finger one last time before slipping it off and placing it on the nightstand. She couldn't help but feel a tear escape down her cheek, a silent testament to her internal struggle. Nina knew she couldn't go on like this forever. She needed answers, clarity, and above all, she needed to know if there was still a future for them. With a heavy heart, she resolved to have the difficult conversation with Darin. It was time to face the reality of their situation, no matter how painful it might be. The question of whether they would ever progress could no longer be ignored, and Nina was determined to find out the truth, for her sake and for her child's.

₁ TRUE PROGRESSION

₁ Many people confuse the true purpose of being in a relationship. It's to grow with the person you love. But what exactly is growth? What does it mean to **grow in love**? Oftentimes we focus on the ceremonial acts of love instead of the true nature of it.

₂ Before you and your man sign legal documents of marriage, before you two spend half of your savings on a wedding, you two better make sure you're growing as people. Growth <u>of</u> Your Relationship and Growth <u>in</u> Your Relationship are two different things. Both are welcome and praised, but they are not the same.

- **Growth *of* Your Relationship is the progression from meeting to marriage. It is the pre-designed order of a relationship. There's a beginning and an end.**

₃ You meet him, you date, and you fall in love which then leads to a more serious relationship. You then marry and have kids. The order is often switched around, but the formula is the same. It's what we've been taught and trained to follow. It's often in our many religious texts as well.

₄ Many people pursue this formula; convinced that reaching the end will lead to happiness. They ignore all the signs along the way, believing that marriage and children will somehow resolve everything. However, reality tells a different story. Marriage isn't the sole objective; genuine growth and love are. Marriage is merely the outcome of nurturing these vital aspects in a relationship, with the ceremonial wedding serving as a public vow to continue this journey together till death.

₅ Unfortunately, many fail to uphold this vow because their relationship lacked these foundational elements from the start. They chased the idea of Growth of the Relationship rather than experiencing true Growth in the Relationship. As a mentor of mine would say, *"A car with no brakes may rush ahead, but it's the slow scenic drive that brings fulfillment."*

- **Growth *in* Your Relationship is when you and your partner grow together as human beings. Your way of life changes for the better because of each other.**

₆ He's there to encourage you to be healthier. You're there to encourage him to start his own business. Or you learn yoga/meditation and teach it to him to help him when he gets upset with work. You two then learn more about it together. You take the best of both your worlds and share it with each other to improve each other's lives. If you're good at drawing and he's good at writing, you two decide to make a children's book. It's helping your significant other drop their cigarette addiction. It's all the things that help you two truly grow as people. That's Growth in Your Relationship. See, there is no limit to it; it's infinite and forever lasting. It's not buying them expensive clothes they couldn't afford before you got there; it's teaching them how local clothing stores get their inventory, which may encourage them to open a store of their own. What value do you bring to this relationship? How do you currently help your man improve his life? What gifts are you sharing with him that add value to him?

7 We always speak about being *as one*. What does that mean? I believe it means we should share our magic with one another. Our gifts and our knowledge are combined to make an explosion of greatness. If he raps and his wife sings, nothing is wrong with teaching her how to deliver some rap bars. Make an album together and share that combined greatness. It's the natural way of life. What do you think your children are? They are a combination of you and him, a bundle of greatness.

8 So, in essence, true progression is the growth of one another through your relationship. That kind of growth is to the end of time. It requires learning and experiencing new life together and there's always something new to add to

your relationship. Marriage again is the public promise that you two will continue this growth until death. Growth *of* the relationship is climaxed once marriage and kids are born. But growth *in* the relationship doesn't end until death because on this planet, *if you're not growing, you're dying.*

₂ CONFUSE HER OUT OF MARRIAGE

₁ Many times, and often unknowingly, men who don't want to get married do subtle things that may cause some confusion in their woman's mind. The idea is to keep her unsure of what she truly wants. It's similar to "The Greatest Trick," which can be found in **JASMINE 2:1** - different scenarios, but the objectives are somewhat the same. Make her love you enough to stay with you but make her unsure about marriage with you.

₂ He would often instill fear about moving forward by adopting a pessimistic outlook on the situation. His comments would echo with negativity, like, *"We can't even correctly ('Blah blah blah') now; imagine if we get married. We have work to do first."* Such seemingly harmless remarks can gradually influence your perspective.

₃ When thoughts of marriage with him arise, you might find yourself with a gut-wrenching feeling of fear.

This instinctual response is deeply ingrained in us—our *Fight or Flight* reaction—a survival mechanism honed during our time in jungles, looking out for wild animals. When faced with perceived danger, our natural inclination is to flee. It's your mind and body's way of protecting you from situations perceived as harmful—unnecessary adrenaline preparing you for either confrontation or escape. Though we've evolved beyond the jungle, this instinct still guides us, even in situations that pose no *real* danger.

4 His constant negative words on the topic of marriage cause the topic to become toxic to your thoughts. Marriage is now attached to danger in your subconscious. Ironically, you may even begin to give reasons and find explanations as to why marriage isn't a good idea. Inside yourself, you may find a new hunger of negativity towards the topic, and you will feed it with negative logic in hopes that the hunger pains go away.

5 Hopefully, your man knows you better than any other guy-which is a good thing. But that also means he knows what makes you tick. He knows his limits with you. He knows what it takes to get broken up with, and he knows what it takes to stay in your good graces. So what does he do? He does what it takes to make you understand that he loves you, but he also creates scenarios and does little things that keep you at bay.

₆ He creates an environment that's not *marriage friendly*. A situation between you two that makes it seem like your marriage wouldn't be ideal. See, women often have a vision of what they want their relationship/marriage to be like. The living conditions, the number of kids, the job schedules, etc. Even if it's not precise, there's usually an outline. Well, if you shared this with your man of many years, he may have a blueprint of what *'not'* to do. So, without saying a word, he can create an environment that causes you to believe, *"We have so much work to do before we're ready."*

₇ Now, on the opposite side of the spectrum, he can also create an environment that feels like you two are married; so much so that you get to a point where you no longer see a reason for actual marriage. When you have everything a married couple has and more, what is the point? These are the types of questions he may ask you, or you may ask yourself. But the questions may be valid and will need a justifiable answer as to why marriage is needed.

₈ So it's *clear* that he can make the relationship *unclear* by clouding your thoughts. This often keeps those marriage thoughts at bay, while your love for him keeps you locked in the relationship box.

3 MAN'S FEAR OF MARRIAGE

1 We have come to a place in life where women are also afraid of marriage as much as men are perceived to be. But there may be different forces tugging on each of us, pulling us away from the altar.

- **Often, men aren't afraid of marriage at all; sometimes, men are simply afraid of the wedding.**

2 It may sound trivial and may be a weak excuse, but one of the world's greatest phobias is speaking in front of a crowd. Well, at weddings, you're doing just that. But not only that, the moment itself is big and can be overwhelming to some men. The *idea* of preparation, rehearsal, fittings, etc. Those things can be turn-offs for some guys, and the magnitude, importance, and expectation of the event can be a bit much for some.

3 But more than anything, the idea of making a public promise is frightening. Everyone at that wedding is expecting him to live by his promise. While he may plan to, having hundreds of people hold him to that promise can have him petrified. If he believes it will not change his love for you, it may seem like a useless occasion to him. He may say, *"Why go through all of this and spend all this money if it won't change how much I love you?"*

- **Marriage has been perceived as the end of something. The end of anything other than pain can be sad.**

4 Let's see if we can find the fallacy in this viewpoint. Marriage is also the *start* of something. But some men will argue that if nothing in the relationship changes, what exactly is it the *start* of? Their ideology is that it's not a new life, new house, or car. It's the same old couple doing the same old things. But by *that* logic, what exactly would this type of man see marriage being the *end* of besides the end of being unmarried? If *he* believes nothing changes within the relationship after marriage, how can it be the end of anything?

5 For most women, marriage has been identified as the ultimate show of love; a man choosing his bride-to-be. She feels special; it's an ego boost for her. Other women envy because they have not yet been chosen.

6 For most men, marriage has been identified as the end of searching. Searching for that one person he wants to spend the rest of his life with. Most men in relationships have never been on a hunt to find that one woman to be with forever. Most guys find a beautiful woman they are attracted to, they get to know her and realize they like her a lot. They become her boyfriend, her man; they fall in love with her and enjoy the time spent with her. This is all great, but he

normally isn't thinking, *"She is the only one for me. This is the best I can find."* It's not always exciting to end the search. Because the curiosity in us makes us wonder...*is this it?*

7 Remember, you don't need a wedding to get married. If marriage is your true goal, you can marry without the ceremony. Some people want a wedding more than they want to be married. It's essential to understand that marriage is a personal commitment to each other, with the <u>option</u> of sharing it with loved ones. It's not for bragging or boasting.

8 If he feels that marriage isn't necessary because *"it won't change anything,"* there shouldn't be a reason **not** to get married. I mean, it won't change anything, right?

4 THE HAYSTACK PARADIGM

1 I want to share a concept called **The Haystack Paradigm**."

2 Imagine you have the chance to reach into a haystack filled with money. Inside, there are a seemingly endless number of $1 bills and a limited number of $100 bills.

3 Here's how it works:

1. COLLECTING $1 BILLS: You can keep all the $1 bills you find. You don't have to put them back, and you can spend them… one at a time. As long as you keep pulling out $1 bills, you can continue collecting more.

2. HANDLING $100 BILLS: If you pull out a $100 bill, you have to put it back unless you decide to stop pulling. When you choose to stop, you can keep that $100 bill but you have to drop all the $1 bills you've collected so far.

₄ Most people would keep collecting $1 bills until they couldn't anymore. Some would grab a $100 bill and exit, knowing it's the highest denomination in the haystack. It all depends on the individual's strategy, i.e. their wants and needs.

$1 BILLS: Easy to collect, keep, and spend immediately. You can pull them out indefinitely, but they can only be used for $1 purchases. This process might get tiring, but you'll always have your $1 bills.

$100 BILL: You can spend it however and whenever you like. Once you grab it, you can stop, as you've got the biggest bill in the stack.

₅ So how does all of this relate to men being afraid of marriage and feeling like it's an end to something? For some men, easy women are like $1 bills. They enjoy the thrill of the chase and the quick satisfaction. The availability seems unlimited, and the fun time while gathered at the haystack creates a competition amongst friends. No one wants to say, *"I quit,"* as it might imply weakness—a distorted perception.

₆ Popular culture, like rap artist, often glorify this lifestyle, making it seem desirable. Young men might grow up believing they should spend most of their life pursuing these quick and easy relationships, only settling down with a long-term partner (the $100 bill) at the end.

₇ The $100 bill represents a wife. Choosing to keep her means the game is over—no more chasing, no more gatherings at the haystack. He now joins other men who have $100 bills but might struggle to find the same enjoyment. He misses the haystack and thinks of all the $1 bills his friends are currently collecting. His competitiveness might drive him back to the haystack, even though he already has a $100 bill.

₈ Some men get so caught up in pursuing new $1 bills that they drop their $100 bill back into the haystack, losing it forever. It all depends on the individual's priorities and decisions.

9 The fear here is about ending one chapter and starting another. It's about leaving behind a life centered on the haystack and entering a new one. It's the fear of uprooting the fragile foundation his ego has been built on; the fear of leaving behind what was once fun and familiar to enter a new life where finding enjoyment might be a challenge.

10 This fear is often described as the fear of growing up. However, growing up is about personal growth, while marriage is about the growth of a relationship. Not wanting a relationship shouldn't be seen as a fear of growing up because people who are single by choice have many valid reasons why they choose to be alone. However, I will say it does take a degree of maturity to protect and provide for a family. A maturity some men have not yet reached in their lives.

5 THE MENTAL WIFE

1 There are many men who have grown up with their idea of what their wife should look like. They have been collecting data on how a wife should act since childhood. Often, their expectations are exaggerated and aren't always realistic.

Due to this, many men don't marry because they haven't found a woman to fit this pre-designed mold. They may find a friend, lover, travel buddy, and someone they spend all day with inside of one woman, but she may not match their pre-conceived idea of a wife. So, while he may love you, you may not be what his subconscious expected. Because of this, he isn't ecstatic about marriage; at least not until he finds someone to match his *Mental Wife*.

₂ Television, movies, music, social media, religion, friends, and family all contribute to what a boy learns about his future wife. He takes the things he likes and creates this woman that he feels is somewhat the perfect wife. He puts a price on his head, in a sense. He tells himself, *"This woman is what it would take for me to settle down and get married."* He doesn't verbalize this sentiment, but by mentally making this claim, he finds himself going through life never fully extending himself and often never fully expressing his love. This is because all the paths of women he has crossed have *not* been the woman he believes he's waiting for. So, in his mind, he's saving himself for her, when often the person he's in love with is right in his face.

₃ As he grows older, this *Mental Wife* changes. She begins to morph as his life develops over time. As he experiences new things, his *Mental Wife* must now understand these new experiences as well. This is why for some men it seems to take a while before they decide to marry their girlfriend. When he experiences new things, it's with his girlfriend. As a result, she now grows as his *Mental Wife* grows. The qualities between the two women begin to line up, which leads him to pop the question.

₄ But when he grows *separate* from his woman, she becomes less and less akin to his *Mental Wife*, making the chances of marriage slim to none.

₅ Again, this *Mental Wife* is based on his upbringing and experiences. So, every man won't see every woman the same. Even if she has what you and I may call great qualities, to someone else they may not be so great at all. Greatness is subjective. While you may believe cooking steak is a wife quality, if his *Mental Wife* is a vegan, your steak recipe is not only useless, but also an opposite to the woman he thinks he should marry.

₆ Women love to ask, *"Can you see yourself marrying me?"* But I'd say the question is, *"Who have you always seen yourself marrying? What are her qualities and what does she look like?"*

₇ If his response is, *"I never really thought about it,"* that means marriage isn't a current goal of his. But that doesn't mean a *Mental Wife* hasn't been formulated in his subconscious; it may just mean he has yet to tap into it. Or he just wants to avoid describing someone who isn't you.

8 If he merely answers, *"You,"* he could be giving you the answer he believes you want to hear. It sounds sweet, but his actions will eventually tell you if he's sincere. A marriage should be in the works.

9 If he describes a woman who is nothing like you, that may explain his hesitation to jump the broom. I feel that you and his *Mental Wife* should have some of the same qualities, more than not. If your relationship has lasted long enough, his *Mental Wife* should have begun to take the image and shape of you. If after 5 years you and she have nothing in common, it may be time to either learn to fit her mold, create more experiences and grow as a couple in hopes to break her mold *or* find another man who has had a different life experience. But this is only if marriage is a deal breaker for you. There could be many reasons for his lackadaisical attitude towards marriage.

10 But at the end of it all, while he may think his mentally generated wife is what he needs, true love is unpredictable; you can't plan or design it.

₆ **WHOSE PAYING FOR OUR LOVE?**

₁ Finances are what often keep men from seeking marriage. Not the marriage license, but the wedding. Traditional wedding rules state that the bride and family are to pay for the ceremony, while the groom and family account for the banquet dinner. I've seen some state that the bride and family are to cover the banquet as well. But from what I've seen, both man and woman together cover the cost. They normally save their money in one account and use that to fund their wedding.

₂ Some men view this as a waste of money, especially when the living conditions aren't where he feels they should be. Some men often feel that the money spent on impressing family and friends with an extravagant wedding can be used to pay off the house you're living in. Or get a new car since yours is always in the shop. Maybe save for an investment that brings you both residual incomes for many years to come instead of on a one-day event.

₃ But this dilemma isn't a marriage issue; it's a wedding issue. Financial excuses for no marriage are based on the wedding ceremony, which normally comes as a package deal for most women who want to get married, but not all women. A courthouse marriage will solve that.

₄ A marriage license is usually quite affordable, but a divorce may not be. Which brings us to another fear men have, divorce. The binding paperwork involved with your love can make things start to seem like a business deal versus growth of a relationship. For years, men have heard stories and seen movies where other gentlemen have been taken advantage of in the court system. Women usually seem to have an advantage in most divorce cases. Even if your man may not have much to give up now, he may be thinking of his future gains. Regardless of the size of the pot, he doesn't want to give up the little bit he does have. Now this fear may just be exaggerated and may be skewed, but it is indeed on the minds of some men.

₅ For those men with a business and/or multiple businesses, their worries may be greater. Even if you directly benefit from his current business, the ideal of marriage with possible divorce looms overhead. Involving the law in your love can cause him distress over thoughts of litigation. Prenuptial agreements could be used if need be; but he maybe afraid to bring that up.

₇ CHANGE FOR BETTER OR WORSE

₁ When a man falls in love with a woman, it's usually a combination of things, one being her physical appearance. The person you get into a relationship with usually has physical features that attracted you. If they improve those features, then that's a plus. That normally sparks a new and necessary lust for your partner. But if those features that he has grown to love begin to fade, it could cause him to be disinterested. While this is just one of many reasons, it's one nonetheless.

₂ Throughout a man's life, he often hears about a woman's main goal being to one day get married. We hear how once these women race to their goal and cross the finish line, they relax and get comfortable because the race is done. For some men, they fell in love with the 'race' in her. In other words, the things she did to present herself as a potential wife, she no longer does because she is no longer a *potential* wife; she *is* a wife.

₃ This scares some men away from marriage. The idea that his woman may, for lack of better words, "*let herself go,*" can frighten him. Many guys have heard from other men about how their wives looked one way and emerged another some time after marriage. This idea is backed by television shows and movies all the same - jokes of a woman who has changed physically after receiving her ring.

₄ While this excuse may sound superficial, it can be avoided by merely exhibiting dedication to your physical health as a lifestyle and not just a temporary activity for a one-time goal. It should also be done as a couple if time permits. Besides, I believe we all should dedicate time to our physical health regardless of our relationship circumstance.

₅ Love is bigger than the physical. Any man who values a woman who exercises and eats clean should embrace that lifestyle himself. If possible, he should find a woman who shares these positive habits. If she doesn't, he could always encourage and motivate her to live healthier. Not for his own personal preference, but for her own health and fitness. Again, *love is bigger than the physical.* You can easily grab a stomach, but you can't always grab love.

8 SHE'S EVERY WOMAN

₁ On a man's journey through life, he may encounter many different women. Each of these women, despite their differences, may offer him something he cherishes. On the surface, this sounds nice, but subconsciously, he may be building his perfect woman. Ladies, you might find yourselves doing this as well. As time passes and relationships end, you add new desired traits to your vision of a future partner. This process parallels, *maturing in life,* where expectations of your life partner evolve with personal growth of yourself.

₂ However, the expectations I want to address here come from the different characteristics of the previous women he dated, slept with and had personal friendships with. These are qualities he collects from previous relationships rather than those developed through his own maturation.

₃ A man dates a woman who rubs his feet; he more than likely believes his wife should soothe his tired soles. He loves a woman who finishes their sex session with oral pleasure; he now expects his future wife to fulfill that intimate role. He partners with a woman who earns six figures; he hopes for a wife who is financially secure. He admires a beauty queen; he imagines his wife with equal grace and allure. Four different women, but in the depths of his mind, they weave into one ideal wife.

₄ In this particular man's mind, he appreciates each woman for what they contribute, and he grows a connection to each contribution. So much so that he can't imagine life without said contributions. Meaning, he has built the perfect woman in his head and anything less in marriage is considered *settling.*

₅ This leaves any woman looking for his hand in marriage at a disadvantage. In love, one grows to love the ways of their partner. In this scenario, he's grown his love within the collection of women he's been with. When faced with these men, they may come across as self-sabotaging.

₆ They might find an attraction that connects <u>them</u> to <u>you</u> as they've done before with previous women. They enjoy this connection and admire you for it. It's part of why he continues to be with you. The problem comes when talks of marriage arise. He begins to assess his *mental wife database* and realizes you don't fill many categories. At that point, he usually looks to exit the relationship.

₇ While I'm speaking of a <u>relationship</u> transitioning to a <u>marriage</u>, this can also apply to <u>dating</u> transitioning to a <u>relationship</u>. For some men, commitment itself isn't awarded unless she fills all the collected characteristics of previous women.

₈ In these situations, you can't force him to accept all of you. But you can give your all and accept the outcome. In order for things to work with *this* man, you will have to adapt all the characteristics of each woman of his past. If they are traits that align with your goals and are upgrades to your life, adding them to your arsenal may not necessarily be a bad thing. But if they are far left from your admirations, ambition, or differ from your way of life, I'd suggest the relationship not be pushed forward. It all depends on how bad you want it.

₉ BREAK THE CURSE

₁ Unfortunately, we also have men who are in serious relationships but are not taking them seriously, and marriage along with being faithful is far from their minds. These men are not ready for a girlfriend, let alone a wife. Sometimes they are pressured into relationships, and other times they lie about their true feelings. They try to convince themselves that they are ready for a relationship, knowing deep down inside that they are not. He may also blame her for badgering him about getting into a relationship when he's already told her he isn't ready for one. This may cause him to get into the relationship just so she will leave him alone about it. These types of relationships aren't grounded on a healthy foundation and may be an even worse marriage, especially if he feels she has pressured him into that marriage.

₂ For these men, marriage is a serious step, and if he doesn't take his current relationship seriously, he's not going to be interested in moving towards more serious ventures.

₃ Also, growing up in a fatherless single-parent household or knowing that your parents were never married as well can mold a young man's mind. Oftentimes, we are just products of our childhood. While little girls may see a lonely mother, little boys can see a free absentee father. When the thoughts of marriage arise in his mind, he thinks, *"My parents never got married and I turned out just fine."* While that may be true, who's to say he wouldn't have been better? But then again, who's to say he wouldn't have been worse?

₄ For these men, marriage is the cherry on top of life; it's nothing necessary or needed to live.

₅ Growing up in a two-parent household can help mold a young boy's choices just the same. Understanding from his birth that two married people in one house is how a house should be. This is embedded early in a young boy's psyche. Getting to know a man's past can help you under-stand his future.

₆ Understand that some fatherless men have learned from their past and do not want to create the same scenario as their father. These men move off the emotions of their past as a way to say **"Fuck you"** to the childhood their father created. They aren't moving in love; they're moving in anger. The results may be the same, meaning you may have a man who wants to be the opposite of his absent father by keeping his family together and getting married. But it may be fueled more by his anger for his father and less fueled by his love for you. Results can be the same, but the motive is blurred. Or we can just look at it as killing two birds with one stone. Break his father's curse and marry the love of his life.

7 Sadly, many men don't want to get married because they expect one woman to equal all the women they've been with. That's just not realistic.

10 TO SUM IT ALL UP

1 Marriage for most men is a big decision. If your man is afraid of making big decisions, marriage may scare him just the same. Go through his life and see all the big decisions he's had to make. If he's not a risk-taker and always takes the safe road, or he just hasn't had any life-changing choices to make, marriage may be too big of a step for him – A big step that might take him some serious time to conquer; especially if it has never been of importance in his childhood and in general.

2 As a woman, what you can't allow yourself to do is drag a man to the altar. Getting married will not solve the problems of your relationship. Marriage happens when you

two *create the formula* for solving your relationship problems.

₃ We now know the difference between Growth of a Relationship and Growth in a Relationship. Marriage without growth inside the relationship can cause what we perceive as stagnation of our relationship. But in actuality, it's stagnation of our lives, and unfortunately, a wedding won't solve that.

₄ So if no-marriage is a deal-breaker for you, make sure you want it for all the right reasons. Make sure you two aren't getting married just because it's *about that time* and it's the *thing to do*. Remember, marriage isn't needed to have love and happiness, but it is an important and symbolic way to announce to the world that you have found your life partner.

Read Nina's story again, what do you think she should do?

"...MANY MEN DON'T WANT TO GET MARRIED BECAUSE THEY EXPECT ONE WOMAN TO EQUAL ALL THE WOMEN THEY'VE BEEN WITH."

- MANUEL V. JOHNSON | NINA 9:7

THE BOOK OF

NYANI

WHY DOES HIS COMMUNICATION SUCK

Nyani was enduring a particularly trying week at work. New management had swept in, reshaping everything in her department and she desperately needed someone to confide in. Naturally, she turned to Brandon, her boyfriend, hoping to hear his comforting words. Yet, true to form, he didn't respond promptly to her text—a recurring pattern that had begun to wear on her. She was growing weary of his seeming indifference and lack of verbal support. Before they officially became a couple, Nyani had made it clear to Brandon that transparency and open communication were non-negotiable for her. She believed in addressing issues head-on and didn't want to be left in the dark about his feelings either. Brandon, however, admitted to struggling with being an open book, often dismissing his behavior as simply being "himself". Neglecting simple things, like neglecting to inquire whether she wanted food on his way to her place.

As their relationship progressed, Brandon's disinterest in nurturing their connection became increasingly clear. Nyani hoped that by directly addressing their issues, Brandon would open up about his true feelings and intentions. She offered him chances to voice any doubts or reservations, even suggesting they take a break if needed. Each time, Brandon reassured her with hollow promises and assurances of commitment, despite his actions consistently failing to align with his words.

On that fateful day at work, Nyani waited anxiously for Brandon's response to her text, seeking reassurance amidst the chaos of her job. Hours passed before he finally replied, suggesting they meet up to discuss something that had been on his mind. With a sinking feeling, Nyani anticipated what was to come. Brandon expressed his belief that their relationship had run its course, buried under the weight of his busy life.

Nyani felt a surge of anger and hurt, not just because their relationship was ending, but because she had known deep down that this moment would come. She couldn't help but think how much pain could have been avoided if Brandon had been more forthright earlier. Masking her disappointment with a composed demeanor, Nyani calmly acknowledged his decision, choosing not to dwell on the unspoken words and unfulfilled promises that hung between them.

Picking up her purse, Nyani couldn't resist a parting comment, her voice tinged with a mix of sadness and frustration.

"Now see, that wasn't so hard, was it?" she said.

Brandon's gaze fell to the floor, unable to meet hers as Nyani walked away, carrying with her the weight of dashed hopes and the ache of a love unreciprocated. In that moment of departure, she mourned not just the end of a relationship, but the loss of the future she had envisioned with him. Yet amidst the sorrow, Nyani found a quiet resolve to move forward. She was determined to heal from the pain of loving someone who couldn't love her back the way she deserved.

₁ OUR WORDS

₁ Having healthy dialogue is vital to having a healthy relationship. But on a more basic level, as humans, we communicate in many ways. *Words* are our thoughts accompanied by our feelings. It takes a certain level of consciousness to speak. Our actions can be incidental or without thought, but our *words* are usually judged by higher standards.

₂ Our words are our bonds. As a New Yorker would say, *"Word Is **Bond**."* The Bible speaks of the word of God; John 1:1 says, *"In the beginning was the Word, and the Word was with God, and the Word was God."* The Law of Attraction teaches us to speak things into existence. So, you see, the power of speech is real. The power of transferring thought from one place to another is important for us to have a society.

₃ Consequently, speech is also important to create relationships. If someone does not know how to express themselves, their partner will not know how to truly interpret what they see in them.

- **Example:** You may come to a party with me because I asked you, but how do you *feel* about this party?

₄ Our words bring a different dynamic that actions don't always speak for. Its little things such as this that I believe hurt relationships: the lack of detailed expression and the absence of important questions. When we have partners who aren't as good with their words, we may have to ask before we assume. Get their side of things instead of just being happy that they've followed us where we asked. Sometimes we're just happy with the fact that they will follow us that we don't care to ask if they think it's a good idea to do so, or if they are simply following us to make us happy.

₅ Our words are important for our expression, and our expression is how our soul breathes. Never be afraid to breathe life into a situation you care about. And also, never be afraid to remain silent on situations that can only stir the pot of negativity.

₂ PROGRAMMED TO BE SILENT

₁ Men are oftentimes bad communicators of emotion, normally because we are often taught that we should deal with our issues internally. In many cases, we are judged and called names for expressing our sadness or pain. Often when men lash out after a bad breakup, they are defined as *"acting like a woman."* This saying comes from a place that ultimately says, *"Expressing distress is only for women."* As a result, many men are programmed to stay tight-lipped.

2 Unfortunately, this programming is unknowingly practiced in relationships. These men keep their words short and their emotions in check the best way they can. Because, well, that's what men are supposed to do, right? This *"suck it up, be a man"* attitude is great until you two break up abruptly and you had no idea that he had a problem. We have to encourage our men to <u>speak what they feel</u>, be strong for our women, but never be afraid to express their doubts, and anxieties.

3 In this new age of social media, our communication reach has expanded, but the quality has diminished. We interact with more people, but these interactions often lack emotion, depth, and detail. The human element is lost when everything is conveyed through a screen. Imagine if every conversation had to be face-to-face. It would bring a different level of expression to our words. But we have phones, and then we discovered texting, and now social media. It's like the difference between a microwave and a conventional oven, or mumble rap versus lyrical hip hop. While every form of communication has its place and no one is forcing us to choose, the allure of easy access is hard to resist.

₄ As a result, many men have become dependent on easy phone access to express their emotions. A man being confident in his tone and presence is becoming rare. We're seeing a decline in the communication skills developed through face-to-face interactions. Essentially, men aren't learning how to speak to women. They aren't building deep connections because it's all digital love now.

₅ When a guy gets your number, it's just symbols on a screen. There's no real human bond connecting him to you. He sends a text, you respond, but he **feels** nothing. He sends another text, and you respond again, but the feeling remains the same. Eventually, you both realize the conversation and newfound friendship are going nowhere. Then, he eventually disappears. This often happens because he never learned or took the time to connect on a deeper level with the actual human behind the screen; you.

₃ ASK THE RIGHT <u>ACTION</u> QUESTIONS

₁ When getting to know a guy, pay attention to how much he's willing to share about himself. Note how often you have to ask, *"So what about you?"* Some men aren't naturally inclined to talk about their lives and often need prompting.

2 If you choose to pursue a relationship with a man who doesn't express himself well, make sure your questions are direct. General questions will receive general answers.

- **Example**: A very general question is, *"Can you see yourself in a relationship with me?"*
- A more direct question is, *"What needs to happen before you're ready for a serious relationship with me?"*

3 The first question will usually get a response like, *"Yeah, I can. You're a great person and very beautiful."*

4 But the second question requires a list of <u>actions</u> that can be <u>tracked</u> and <u>checked off</u>. If his response to the second question is, *"I don't know, I never thought about it,"* then it's clear that a relationship is not on his mind. So make sure your questions require *actionable responses.*

5 Instead of asking, *"Do you still want this relationship to work?"* ask, *"What are you going to do differently to ensure this relationship continues to work?"*

6 A list of actions is now needed. If he doesn't have a response, how can you expect him to make things right? He doesn't know how to or hasn't even thought about where to begin.

₄ **AGGRESSIVE RESPONSES**

₁ Oftentimes, men will avoid simple conversations because they know it may lead to a complex argument. If you have aggressive communication practices, he may not be eager to deal with what comes with expressing himself to you. It's kind of like our teenagers. They regularly keep things from us because they feel that we won't understand their stance and they don't want to get hassled about the topic, so they much rather not even mention it.

₂ Be **Conversational**, not **Confrontational**.

₃ Make sure you are welcoming to his opinions and thoughts. When someone expresses themselves to you, shooting them down or rejecting their assertion can hinder communication moving forward. Imagine working up the nerve to do public speaking for the first time, only to get booed off stage. For many, that will be their last time attempting public speaking. So make sure your response is real, but respectful. There's a difference between being *"real"* and being *"rude."*

₄ If you ask your man about his feelings and he shares something troubling, it wouldn't be wise to say, *"You need to man up and deal with it."* You need to encourage the man in him, not belittle him.

₅ A more supportive reply would be, *"I believe in you. I know you can tackle this issue. I wouldn't be with you if I didn't believe that."* Then, you can work on problem-solving together. If you can't offer any help, why would anyone want to share their issues with you?

₆ Speak to the man within him that you want to see come out. If you address him as a mother would, you'll awaken the child attitude inside. But if you speak to him as his woman, his unwavering support, you can summon the grown man dwelling within him.

₅ THE QUIET WORLD OF TEXTING

₁ We spend much of our time with our heads down in our phones. Our mouths are closed, our bodies stationary, yet we are communicating, nonetheless. Text messaging has helped us multitask more efficiently, but it has also made our communication less effective.

₂ I believe we have reached a point where we are becoming more isolated in society while simultaneously opening up to strangers. You become better at whatever you practice and worse at what you practice less. When we habitually send fragments of our thoughts in short texts, we begin to think and communicate in fragments.

₃ We save our full thoughts and instead we use phone numbers, not to talk, but to text. People send texts *online*, exchange numbers, only to continue texting *offline*. Often, the first words spoken are minutes before meeting: *"I think I'm outside your house."* We are grooming ourselves to be worse communicators. If Communication is *Key,* we may have locked ourselves out of love's *door*.

₄ Many men seem naturally brief when discussing topics they aren't fond of. Texting their way through conversations is ideal, allowing them to ignore topics they don't want to address and focus on those they do. This practice leads to *selective expression*, only addressing what they're comfortable with instead of what needs to be discussed. Ultimately, it creates someone who doesn't express himself to his partner when it's needed or expected.

₆ I'LL DEAL WITH IT LATER

₁ We should all practice addressing issues as they come. Leaving your significant other in the dark about your emotions can lead to the <u>death</u> of your relationship. When you let cancer grow, it sometimes gets so enormous that it can't be stopped. Well, this works with our cancerous relationship issues as well. Not only does expressing how you feel help the relationship, it also relieves tension within yourself.

₂ Men who are natural procrastinators can be known for putting off important conversations. This can lead to him harboring a list of relationship dislikes while leaving you without the opportunity to correct these issues. These types of men will let problems build until they topple over on you, forcing you to address 10 issues at once in hopes of saving the relationship.

₃ Putting off an issue doesn't solve the issue; it merely pushes the end zone further back which causes you to have to run further to score a touchdown. Eventually, you're going to get tired of running.

₄ While it might be ideal to avoid procrastinators, if you find yourself in a relationship with one, it's crucial to ensure he is aware of his actions or lack thereof. The first step toward making any change is recognizing that there is an issue.

₅ Providing concrete examples of how his procrastination has negatively impacted you, him, and the relationship can help him clearly see the consequences of his behavior. This clear illustration of his missteps can serve as a powerful motivator for change, helping him grasp the importance of addressing his procrastination.

₆ He'll make the proper changes I'm sure…. when he gets to it.

₇ **SPEAK UP**

₁ Transparency is vital to maintaining a healthy relationship. Being 'One' with someone means being of 'One Mind'. You and your significant other should share a common understanding. This doesn't mean thinking the same or reading each other's minds, but rather communicating thoroughly with one another. This is why it's often said that you should marry your best friend. Marry someone you can confide in, not hide your secrets from. Marry someone you can share your feelings with, not be in your feelings about.

₂ For women, regular communication is a necessity for comfort. For men, it's more of a tool to convey a point. Often, in the beginning of a relationship, he may be very conversational, driven by the mission to win you over. But once he has, he might feel less compelled to keep the conversations flowing. To him, small talk can seem pointless once the relationship is in motion.

₃ It's not that he doesn't love you or thinks you're not worth talking to; he just prefers to speak when he feels he has something important to say. If he has something significant on his mind, he will share it. However, what's important to him may differ from what's important to you. While you might feel he's not sharing enough, he may believe he's sharing all that's necessary.

8 **FINAL WORDS**

1 Ask direct questions to get direct answers and pose action questions that require specific responses. Be accepting of his words, not dismissive. Recognize that technological advances have trained many of us to be distant, making communication abundant but second-rate.

2 Its common for men to be less communicative than women. However, if he struggles to express himself verbally, he should compensate by being a good listener. Effective communication involves both speaking and listening.

3 While you may excel at sharing your feelings, ensure you're equally attentive when he opens up about his emotions.

4 Ultimately, it's crucial to keep your partner informed and engaged. When someone sees you as a best friend, they tend to share more openly. Friends offer mental comfort, while lovers provide physical comfort. Achieving both roles—

lover and friend—creates a unique and deeply fulfilling connection, like a dance where each step brings you closer to
true unity.

Read Nyani's story again, what do you think the problem was?

"... IF COMMUNICATION IS *KEY,* WE MAY HAVE LOCKED OURSELVES OUT OF LOVE'S *DOOR.*"

- MANUEL V. JOHNSON | NYANI 5:3

THE BOOK OF

TIARA

WHY GET INTO A RELATIONSHIP IF YOU'RE GOING TO CHEAT ON ME

T iara slammed the door of her apartment's gym, the resounding thud echoing through the empty hallway. Without missing a beat, she jumped onto the treadmill and began her assault on the machine. Her feet pounded against its belt, each step a desperate attempt to channel her raging frustrations into something productive. Working out had always been her sanctuary, her escape in times of emotional turmoil, but this time, the storm inside her was unlike any she had faced before. The man she'd given her all to, had given all his manhood to another woman. At 28, Tiara was experiencing the sting of betrayal for the first time in her life, and the pain was almost unbearable. Tiara and Ronny had been a couple for three years; both with child from a previous re-lationship. They had been planning to move in together, to blend their lives into a semblance of a family, but now those plans were shattered.

Tiara couldn't understand why he would betray her trust. She had done everything he asked for, and more. She cooked his favorite meals, she made love to him whenever he was in the mood, and she never nagged him. What baf-fled her most was that she always felt he never matched her efforts in the relationship. If anyone should have cheated, it should have been her, she thought. She saw no reason for him to stray, but he had.

She discovered his infidelity through his text messages. Normally, she respected his privacy, but on this day, a nag-ging intuition led her to check his phone. What she found were conversations and pictures that made it clear he was involved with another woman. When she confronted him, he tried to deflect, focusing the conversation on her trust issues and even questioning her love for him. *"You must be looking for a reason to end this relationship anyway,"* he had said.

After a lengthy argument, Ronny finally admitted to some of her accusations. He basically took a plea for a lesser charge. She didn't convict him of first-degree cheating; instead, he was guilty of *inappropriate behavior with intent to perform a sexual act, and relationship disrespect*. This earned him some time in the doghouse but not a life sentence without her. She loved him, and after three years together, she had shared more experiences and laughs with him than with her two previous boyfriends combined. She didn't want to lose her soul mate after investing so much into the relationship. So, she forgave him. *"Nobody's perfect,"* she mulled over, convincing herself that this was the right decision.

But Ronny hadn't learned his lesson. A year after this first incident, Tiara discovered he had slept with his daughter's mother, Marie. Despite all the derogatory things he had said about his baby mother, he still went back to lay with her. This time, the betrayal cut even deeper. Tiara felt stabbed in the back, because Ronny knew about the hurtful things she had said about Tiara, and he still allowed Marie to have one up on her.

She couldn't take it anymore. She had seen too many friends live in fear of being cheated on and she wanted no part of that endless paranoia. She decided to end her relationship with Ronny and move on with her life. It was clear he wasn't ready to be faithful, so she let him go.

Two years after their breakup, Ronny contacted Tiara on social media with a simple *"Hi."* She was in a good place in her life, so she responded. A conversation ensued, and they exchanged numbers. Days went by without any further contact, but this new interaction sparked Tiara's curiosity. *"What if things could be different?"* she thought. But then, she took a deep breath and deleted his number from her inbox.

But that didn't stop her mind from wandering. *"Why had he cheated?" "Why can I still see us as a couple?"* Just as these thoughts swirled in her head, her phone buzzed with a message alert…. It was Ronny.

₁ **PROGRAMMED TO CHEAT**

₁ Since we were young boys, we've been subconsciously bombarded with the idea that sleeping with women is the number one masculine thing to do; along with stuff like driving fast cars, playing sports, knowing how to fix things around the house, and providing for our kids. While the latter ideas don't seem far-fetched, they aren't as highlighted as having multiple women.

₂ Oftentimes, the cool guy on television is the guy with two girls on his shoulder. In music, primarily rap and commercial rock music, having multiple women and sleeping with someone else's woman is honored. This is the mindset we are programmed to believe.

₃ Now, if a guy wants to be single and sleep with who he pleases, I have no issue with that. That's his choice, and not everyone deserves to be in a relationship or is prepared for one. It becomes a concern when that man decides to commit to a relationship but still has intentions of sleeping with who he wants. Before committing to a woman, he must first shed that programming. The initial step is recognizing that this programming *has* influenced him and may *still* be influencing him.

₄ Young boys who grew up around misguided family members, like older brothers, cousins, or uncles, have often been pressured into having sex as fast and with as many girls as possible. Both young girls and boys experience some sort of pressure, but I don't believe that adult women are encouraging young girls to sleep with everyone at a higher rate than adult men encouraging young boys to sleep with everyone. As a result, young boys grow into young men whose main objective is to sleep with as many women as possible.

₅ Sleeping with more and more women is encouraged as a boy grows, and the number of women he sleeps with defines how much of a man he is. He is rewarded for sleeping with more than one woman, almost as women are rewarded for sleeping with fewer men. As teens, boys embody this, and their path of bedding multiple women is set.

₆ This mindset plays into cheating simply because, once he stops trying to sleep with multiple women, subconsciously he may feel he's no longer a man. The ultimate path of manhood planted in his brain a decade ago is now being erased. *Erased for what? For one woman?* This is why, when boys often get into relationships, their friends begin to make fun of them for caving in or getting off the path of "manhood." As we grow into men, you don't see other men teasing their friends for getting into relationships; it's accepted as we mature.

7 Being that we as boys have been programmed to believe that having multiple women makes us who we are, once in a relationship, we sometimes have a hard time breaking that thought process. We also have a hard time explaining it. Have you ever had a guy try to explain *why* he cheated? He is either confused with a bunch of *I don't knows,* or he starts making seemingly ridiculous claims like, *"I'm lonely at night,"* even though you're the one that has to beg to see him every night. The reason he has trouble explaining what's really happening is because he doesn't know.

8 So while he may love you, he may want to be with you, and he may want to grow a family with you, not sleeping with multiple women can almost feel like he is losing part of who he is in the process. Imagine building your foundation on a ridiculous ideology and then, because you commit to a woman, you have to destroy that foundation you're standing on. If a man has not built a *real* foundation in life, if he has not found what makes him a man, he'll continue to hold onto the idea that being promiscuous is how he exhibits his manhood.

9 **Fellas, let me talk to you for a minute.**

If the only thing that makes you a man is sleeping with multiple women, you, my guy, have been misguided. Quite the opposite is true. A man chooses his woman and respects her because he only picks women he believes are *worth his respect*. If a man chooses to chase and sleep with a woman who isn't worth his respect, what does that make him? It makes him a man who, too, isn't worth that same respect. Being a masculine man takes a certain level of strength. One thing that illustrates great strength is <u>discipline</u>.

10 Yes, the word most humans fear: discipline. A man with self-control and discipline displays *high-level masculinity*. Most people have a hard time controlling their urges, but a man who can conquer such a feat should reward himself before anyone else can. Always remember, taking a woman who's been broken into multiple pieces and assisting her in putting herself back together shows more masculinity than sleeping with multiple women behind their backs. I'm not suggesting it's a man's job to completely fix broken women. I'm merely pointing out the two differences in building women and destroying women and how masculinity should be interpreted within those actions.

11 Again, I can't knock a man who is single and wants to sleep with many women—I understand the freedom of it

all. But do not let that define your manhood. Don't let that be the foundation of what makes you a man to be respected. Especially if you feel the women you are sleeping with aren't worthy of **your** respect.

₁₂ The problem is being in a relationship and continuing to have that mindset, believing that you have to continue to sleep with these women. If the woman you chose to be in a relationship with is worthy of your respect, you should give it to her, and if you don't, what does that make you? <u>A man must be strong and show discipline.</u> Can you, as a man, show strength and self-control?

₂ LUST FOR NEW WOMEN

₁ When it comes to cheating, the allure of *newness* can greatly influence a man's decision-making. As relationships mature, people sometimes begin to take each other for granted. Even though everything they need is right there, an *internal* sense of something missing can make it seem like the relationship itself is lacking. This often leads them to seek fulfillment outside the relationship, despite the root of their dissatisfaction being internal rather than external.

Sometimes looking for external solutions for internal problems can be as hollow as chasing your own shadow.

₂ This can be connected to men in the area of sex. He can have the best sex partner he's had in years or ever, but because she's already in his possession, there's nothing left to conquer. The need for something new arises. Remember, we're talking about men that feel sleeping with many women makes them alpha males. So the need to conquer a woman makes him feel achieved.

₃ When a man's foundation and self-defining mold is based on how many women he's been with, there will continuously be this urge for new women, a new mountain to climb to get that rush of *success* again. This urge doesn't go away just because he loves you; to him, those are two separate things. This is why there are many *levels* to love. Being that this urge to be what he perceives to be *a man* is still there, he cheats. He continues to sleep with other women because, through his eyes, this is part of his existence.

₄ For some men, they view sex with the same woman as eating the same type of meat every day. He may view sex with you as eating steak, and daily there's a different type of steak on his plate: New York strip, filet mignon, rib eye, T-bone steak, etc. But at the end of the day, it's steak. It may be a better-quality meat than others, but it's often said that too much of anything is bad. So while a simple question to him may be, *"Which meat is better, and which meat would you rather have?"* he will probably pick steak over a pork chop. But once he realizes he can never have a pork chop again, it may cause him to panic. He will either both adapt and come to realize that there are a variety of sauces available to *spice* up the steak. Or it may cause him to plan on having his *steak and eating his pork chop too.*

₃ WHY MEN SLEEP WITH LESS ATTRACTIVE WOMEN

₁ When it comes to the women he chooses to sleep with, many wives and girlfriends alike are shocked. I've heard women say, *"If you're going to cheat, at least let her be worth it."* Questioning why he took a step backwards to sleep with someone she feels isn't on her level, asking why men cheat with *"ugly"* women more than not.

₂ Well, if his goal is to conquer a new woman and not start a relationship with her, her looks, her job, how many kids she has, her car and her house are all irrelevant to him. She's a woman and his goal is to sexually conquer her.

₃ Just because she may be viewed as *ugly*, doesn't mean she's easy in bed. Just because she hasn't found a great paying job like you, doesn't mean she's easy in bed. Just because she's had 7 kids, doesn't mean she's easy in bed. It only takes having sex 7 times to have 7 kids (with exception to having twins). So technically we don't know how many times she has had sex and with how many partners. And even if her *body count* is high, his goal is to add her to the list.

₄ If you see a $100 bill and a $5 bill on the ground next to one another, would you not grab the $100 bill AND the $5 bill even though it's substantially smaller? So in essence, she could still very well be something he feels he had to conquer.

₅ But in actuality, she doesn't even have to play hard to get in order for him to feel like he conquered her. The mere fact that she gave herself to him is an accomplishment. In his mind, if she's hard to get, he gets a gold medal; if she's easy, he takes the bronze. Either way, he medals in the situation. So while you may feel she isn't worthy, she's right up his alley.

₆ If she is in fact easy to sleep with, that can also be appealing because he doesn't have to spend time trying to convince her to sleep with him. She'll more than likely be ok with him having a girlfriend as well.

7 Also, he can probably sleep with her anytime and anywhere. An easy woman is perceived as being more flex-ible to his needs and scheduling. That's a perfect situation for a cheater.

8 Women often tell me that they are confident that their man isn't cheating because he doesn't have the time, or he doesn't have the energy to meet another woman. To that I say… it only takes 30 minutes out of his day to sleep with another woman. That's one traffic jam excuse away. He can claim he's going to the store for something, something he already told his side chick to go to the store and get. He then stops by his side chick's house for a quick sex session, grabs the items and comes home to you. Tells you traffic was slow due to an accident, the lines were long, he got caught by a train or if he timed it correctly, he doesn't need an excuse. Especially if he leaves while you're busy.

9 I say all that to say, if his other woman knows and accepts his situation, he can make things happen very easily on the way home from work. Leave work early with a fake sick-ness, go to her house, come home drained and tell you he's not feeling well. I've seen situations where a guy's side chick has come to his job and has had sex with him in the car.

When two people truly want to have sex, they will by any means. And it seems the more *risqué* she is, the less *risky* the situation is.

I know you're asking, *"But why would he 'risk losing me for someone who can't replace me?"*

10 Excellent question, but here's the problem:
He doesn't believe he will get caught. Primarily because he believes he's smarter than he actually is. It's like that old saying that says men don't like to ask for directions while driving when it's clear they're lost.

11 He has an overabundance of confidence. Often this confidence grows greatly from cheating so many times before. This can lead to him getting sloppy after a while and driving him to think he has you figured out. In his mind it's not much of a risk.

12 Keep in mind, we're just talking about sex, not a thoughtful detailed situation for him. He's thinking about satisfying an urge right now, not his future. Most men don't think of their future when they have sex. So he will more than likely not be thinking of the *future risk* of losing you.

13 Sometimes the type of women a man sleeps with shows you the type of man he is. You just may be above his

level and the women he's sleeping with may be on his level. Mentally they could both be simple-minded individuals regardless of their status in society. If he doesn't recognize your value, he may believe she can replace you. His perception may be an inaccurate analysis of you.

14 When a man gets to a point where he doesn't care if he loses you, getting caught can be worth the risk. Keep in mind that just because he was caught sleeping with her, doesn't mean he has to be in a relationship with her if him and you break up. He may not even view it as choosing *"her over you."* He probably views it as *"him with you"* or *"him single."* And again, if he has already mentally left the relationship, getting caught just may be his 2 weeks' notice before he quits. Losing you isn't a risk at all, it was inevitable.

15 Now, <u>why</u> he mentally checked out of the relationship is a different topic.

4 SEX IS TREATED AS AN AWARD

1 In most cases, the options for sex are higher for women than they are for men. The average woman can get hit on three times in one day, while the average man can go three months without getting hit on once. So for most men, having

a woman express her attraction to him without notice is a great feeling and it's **addictive**.

₂ As a result, it makes it *rare,* and rarity is usually valuable. The less of it there is, the more we want it. A man who has ten women trying to sleep with him every day isn't going to value sex as much as a guy who has two women trying to sleep with him once a year.

₃ Understand this, even though the guy who has ten women trying to sleep with him daily doesn't value sex as much, he will still sleep with as many women as he can. *Why?* Because the opportunity was there. The "value" of sex doesn't matter.

₄ There are so many men who don't even care about the woman they are sleeping with; sometimes they don't even find her attractive. They do it just because it's available. Just to be able to say, *"Yeah, I slept with her."* They view it as a notch under their belts - an **achievement.**

₅ Let's say you're a racecar driver and you want to be known as the greatest driver of all time. You're going to need the accolades and stats to prove this. You're going to need to win the big races and in impressive fashion. But just the same, you're going to need the little races as well. Every award counts - every trophy sits on the shelf.

₆ When a guy views sleeping with a woman as an achievement to be excited about, it doesn't really matter the level of the award. All the awards make his trophy case look better. Even if individually some of the awards are from meaningless races.

₇ Who doesn't like awards? Who doesn't enjoy that feeling of accomplishing something, we all do. Serotonin, oxytocin, dopamine, and endorphins are responsible for our happiness as humans. When sex with a woman activates any of these, particularly dopamine which lies within the *pleasure-reward system,* accompanied with a rush of testosterone, an addiction to that feeling can form. Not necessarily an addiction to the actual feeling of sex, but an addiction to women choosing him for sex. He feels *special* because he has been chosen, and getting into a relationship doesn't always make that addiction to being *chosen* go away.

₈ Yes, his girlfriend chose to be <u>committed </u>to him (which should also be special) but he knows many other women would commit to him just the same, so commitment doesn't necessarily make him feel truly special. Especially if his girlfriend's previous relationships ended because her boyfriend at the time cheated on her. That means in essence she's with her new boyfriend because the last guy stepped out on her. She didn't just choose the new boyfriend over the old one, she was hurt by the old boyfriend and so she left him. If the old boyfriend was faithful, she would have never chosen the new boyfriend. I know it's a superficial way to look at it, but when someone is searching for justification, they'll grasp at anything.

₉ But when a woman chooses him for sex, regardless of her reasons, it still activates the chemicals in his brain. He still feels rewarded because since a kid he has been programmed to believe he's *receiving* something special and not *giving* something special. If men stopped viewing sex as *receiving vagina* and started to view it as *giving penis*, many men would value their bodies more.

₅ DOESN'T KNOW WORTH

₁ The value men place on the <u>vagina</u> is <u>high</u>, and that's fine. The problem arises when the value they place on their <u>penis</u> is <u>low</u>. Many men view the vagina as a $100 bill. So, of course, when offered, they're going to take it. But they view their own penis as a $1 bill, so naturally, an exchange of 100 for 1 is always going to be worth the trade. They have no problem giving themselves out to women because losing a dollar isn't going to stop their day, but missing out on $100 just might.

Rate Her Value

₂ When rating women on a scale from 0 to 100, their value can vary depending on how many times he has slept with her. At one point she may have been worth 100, after a couple of years of sleeping with her, her value drops. So even though she may be a better person than another woman, her value has fallen a few notches on his list due to the fact that he has conquered her over and over again. But to another man who has never been with her, her value is still 100.

₃ Not all women start off at 100, which can be tricky. Some women start at 80, and from there, she drops down depending on her S.U.R. or *"Sexual Usage Rate."* If a woman has slept with a friend of his or someone he views as being beneath him, either of those scenarios can lower her value before he sleeps with her.

₄ On the contrary, for many men, a woman who is related to an enemy or is the girlfriend/ex-girlfriend of a guy he doesn't like, those scenarios can boost her value. A married woman or a woman in a committed relationship can also appear more valuable to the men who see sex with many women something to be proud of.

₅ You must understand that this isn't just about sex; this is about <u>ego</u>. This is about his false belief that conquering a woman sexually is what makes him a man. So the idea that he has conquered a woman who is with another man is the ultimate achievement for him. It's one thing to claim land that no one owns. It's another thing to take someone's land by force and then claim it. To the egotistical, that's a feeling of *power and dominance*. And we know that power can be addictive.

6 When a man begins to value his penis as he values the vagina, he'll begin to show concern for who he gives it to. He'll grow standards as to who he feels is worthy, just as women seem to do with their vagina. Men must learn to be stingy with their penis and tell some women, *"No."* If most women are worth your penis, your penis isn't worth much.

6 SHE'S FAMILIAR

1 From my time spent answering email stories from confused women who've been cheated on, I've found that many cheating situations are created with women the guy has been involved with before he met his current woman. This is largely due to the level of comfort he has with her. They've been through quite a bit, and she's seen girlfriends like you *come* and *go* before. Or maybe she is a previous girlfriend looking for a second chance or, better yet, revenge for being cheated on by him — her plans may be to expose his infidelity.

Either way, if deep down inside she wants him, she's going to cater to all his needs. She's going to be extra sexual in bed and overly understanding; feed his ego. These are the things that keep him coming back for more.

2 Life seems easier with her because she doesn't have to deal with the idea of him cheating, so she doesn't question him. He feels pressure with you and none with her. Not because you're doing something wrong, but what he's feeling is the pressure of the relationship — the pressure of fulfilling expectations. With her, there are no expectations, only the expectation is to perform in bed. Pleasing his woman and pleasing his side chick are two different tasks. One requires a list of things, and the other requires a time and place for sex. When they're familiar with one another, it makes cheating much easier.

3 If she's an ex-girlfriend, her goal could merely be to make herself feel worthy again in his eyes. If she still loves and values him, although he's with you, sex with him makes her feel wanted even more. Experienced male cheaters know this and take advantage of the ex-girlfriend's game — he sleeps with her and leaves it at that. And her dreams of getting back together are cooked.

4 Inexperienced cheaters may actually leave their relationship for their ex. Only to later find that nothing has changed

between them. In fact, his ex might be a worse fit for him now. Whatever issues they had before weren't solved by his recent cheating with her. All she did was go from *girlfriend* to *side chick*, back to *girlfriend*. His urge for a side chick is still there, and she helped feed it this entire time.

5 When the woman he cheats with is familiar, she's usually been around for many of his previous girlfriends. She's been *"battle-tested"* so to speak. She finds pleasure in being his relief from you while finding her relief <u>with him</u>.

6 Men with good sex usually cheat more. This is due to women in his past not wanting to let go of his sexual greatness. She probably believes she can't find another man as good as him, so she sticks by his side. Her willingness to stick around just because of his penis boosts his sexual ego, so he allows her to stay in his life to continue to hear that particular praise from her.

7 THE GREAT MALE SEXUAL EGO

1 Men with good sex have been constantly told they have good sex. It has fed their ego for years, and now they've grown to love the praises these many women sing. It becomes an addiction to please women. But pleasuring the same woman grows old because once he's proven he's great,

he has no desire to continue to prove it to her. He needs a new woman to prove his greatness to.

₂ You may tell him how great he is, but because you're in love, he might see your words as biased and less valuable on this topic. However, someone he just met is the perfect person to test his pleasure skills on. If for nothing else, just to see if those skills are as great as he's always been told. *"How will she react to me in bed?* Is how he views it.

₃ Sometimes women believe that men who pay attention to detail in bed are doing so out of love for her. While that often plays a part, in many cases, she may be dealing with a man who has just perfected his sexual craft. He cares about his performance because it boosts his ego when he's congratulated for great sex. So every time he performs, he makes sure he does a great job. Primarily it's because the purpose of having sex in the first place for him is to feed the sexual ego, not necessarily to simply ejaculate.

₄ Ever met a man who didn't really care if he ejaculated? And instead, he just wanted to make sure you orgasm? His ego will be fed from your praise of his performance. He obviously would *want* to cum, but if he didn't, he's not upset.

₅ These men will appear to be more giving in bed than you're used to. They are big on performance and in need of praise.

If your man is performance-driven, you may want to give him all the praise in the world — his ego needs it from somewhere. It can make him live up to your praises, thus improving your overall sexual experience with him. But again, if he's a cheater, your words may be viewed as biased from his perspective; due to your words being drenched in love.

₆ After a while in your relationship, great sex may become the norm. You may enjoy it, but your enthusiasm towards it may have naturally dwindled. He may need his sexual ego stroked. If you aren't doing it, he may feel the need to find it elsewhere. Usually, the woman he cheats with is the one who strokes his ego best. Not solely with her words, but with how loudly she moans during sex, her multiple orgasms, her constant harassment for more sex, her *"freakiness"* in bed, and of course, her texting and telling him how good it is.

₇ These situations are unfair to you, the girlfriend/wife, because there's so much more in your relationship you have to praise him on. His father skills, how he handles stressful situations, the problem-solving advice he gives you, etc. It's so much more than sex, so it becomes an afterthought sometimes for you. But for the other woman, all she has to focus on is sex and nothing more. While you may be akin to Walmart, offering a broad range of options, sometimes it's best to visit a specialty shoe store to find exactly what you're looking for.

8 BEFORE HE'S READY TO SETTLE DOWN

1 As explained earlier, many guys' mentality is to have sex with as many women as possible. It begins as a young teen and is reinforced as he gets older through friends, male relatives, music, and movies. This eagerness to want to be perceived as a *"real man"* is not easily cut off. It is normally brought into relationships and often marriages if not shut down beforehand.

2 Shutting it down doesn't normally happen until the guy goes through a few stages:

- **First stage** is when he stops chasing/looking for new women to have sex with. He's not asking for phone numbers anymore. He's to the point where he lets women pursue him instead, but still makes himself easily available.

- **Second stage** is when he isn't excited about new sex; he's had plenty. If more women come, then so be it, if not, he knows he can go get some if he wants some. Now he picks and chooses who he sleeps with very sparingly. He becomes picky with the women he beds. He's no longer easily available to every woman. He doesn't feel the need to sleep with all of them.

- **Third stage** is when he has about two or three women he sleeps with regularly for the year. He doesn't have the patience to *get to know* new women just to sleep with them anymore. He becomes lazy in the dating department. So he keeps these same two or three women around. If he prematurely gets into a relationship, these women are normally the side chicks that have stuck around.

- **Fourth stage** is when he's tired of dealing with multiple women; their emotions and attitudes. He wants just one woman. At this stage, sex can become boring sometimes. He has the one he wants, but his drive isn't as strong as it once was. After years of slowly shutting down the urges of new sex, it actually cut some of his urge for sex altogether. Some men can still have a pretty good sex drive in this stage, especially if his significant other continues to turn him on. A lot of guys without a high sex drive get married because one woman can fill their cup of sex. They know only one woman will satisfy them because their lust is low. On the bad side, low lust can spill over into his marriage. Often the wife is left feeling

146 Know Thy Man

unwanted in bed. His lust for her is unfortunately reduced as well. Testosterone and libido are not what they once were.

₃ Guys who get married at the **First Stage** have a higher probability of cheating. Their lust is high, so their women feel wanted in bed and are usually highly pleased. Guys who get married at the **Fourth Stage** have a lower probability of cheating, but their lust meter is also lower, so occasionally their women aren't as pleased in bed.

₄ Often women find themselves attached to men despite signs telling her to leave. I expressed this very thing in the **ANGIE 1:1** section of this book. I speak about why women may feel attached to situations they don't want to be attached to. Optimism, sex, and ego are the three main attachments:

1. Being optimistic that he will change for the better because he does so many other things right — a father to his child, etc.
2. Fear that another sex partner <u>can't</u> replace him.
3. Ego being the desire to win. Women who don't want to let another woman have her man feel as though it's a competition, and winning said competition is important, even if the grand prize is a bag of shit.

5 Look for a man who **values discipline**. Those who can control their impulses are typically better at resisting temptations like cheating. If he already demonstrates discipline in managing other temptations, such as resisting a donut on a diet, it suggests he has a better chance of self-control to resist temptations in relationships than someone who can't stop himself from anything.

Read Tiara's story again, what do you think the problem was?

"...IT ONLY TAKES 30 MINUTES OUT OF HIS DAY TO SLEEP WITH ANOTHER WOMAN. THAT'S ONE TRAFFIC JAM EXCUSE AWAY."

- MANUEL V. JOHNSON | TIARA 3:8

THE BOOK OF
LEXI

WHY IS EVERY RELATIONSHIP A BAD RELATIONSHIP

I t was over. Lexi had just ended her two-year relationship. Another guy she thought had potential
turned out to be a complete screw-up. Time after
time, Lexi found herself in the same heart-wrenching situation. She'd meet a guy who seemed to embody many of
her favorite qualities, who also promised commitment and
sincerity. They wouldn't just use her for a fling; they'd talk
of a future together. Some even seemed more eager for a
relationship than she did. But inevitably, it all would fall
apart. Lexi always questioned if there was any love left

after each heartbreak. And despite finding new potential partners, each attempt only added to her pain rather than healing her wounded heart like many women in her position, doubt began to creep in. She scrutinized her own thinking and reevaluated her standards, wondering if they were too stringent. Eventually, she concluded that perhaps it wasn't entirely her fault, but rather her choice in men.

Her last relationship was with a guy she had known for over a year. Elijah had always flirted with her, though she never took him seriously because he didn't fit her usual type. Despite his charm and good looks, his lifestyle didn't align with hers. Yet he made her laugh and spoke passionately about his goals and interests. In her eyes, he had potential, so when he finally asked her out, she agreed. They clicked. Fresh from a draining relationship, she eagerly embraced his everyday humor as a source of joy.

Months passed, and they became an official couple. Initially, everything was wonderful. But as time went on, cracks began to appear. Elijah's lifestyle, which she had purposely overlooked before, became a growing concern. He resisted seeking stable employment, his lies multiplied, and inconsistencies surfaced.

Once again, Lexi found herself in familiar despair: another man she had invested her heart in turned out to be a disappointment. Despite stepping out of her comfort zone, hoping for a different outcome, she faced yet another heart break. Now, Lexi asks herself with a heavy heart, "*Am I the problem?*"

₁ **WHY DID YOU MISS THE RED FLAGS?**

₁ When it comes to building a relationship, it takes two sides. There is no right or wrong side; they're just different perspectives—yours and his. Sometimes we meet people, and perhaps because they're attractive, we try to discover other qualities we like in them. It's natural for us as humans to attach and multiply. So, once they pass our attractiveness test, we look to find qualities that will allow us to connect successfully.

₂ Often during this process, we ignore their flaws because we're not looking for reasons <u>not</u> to be with them; we're searching for reasons <u>to</u> be with them. As the Bible's **Matthew 7:7** says, *"...seek and ye shall find."*

₃ When our mind is focused on forming a connection, we subconsciously look for things that bond us, all while our brain overlooks the potential disconnects. It's like when you start dating someone with a certain car, and suddenly, you see that car everywhere you go. Your mind is truly powerful; when you unconsciously direct it to find something, it looks until it finds it. Your brain knows *you* better than you know yourself.

₄ Initially, you see all the good traits because your attachment radar is *on*, and you overlook the bad traits because your detachment radar is *off*. This allows you to get close to someone who may have potential but could also be a poor match. The natural desire for a relationship to flourish can suspend <u>critical thinking</u>. In other words, you believe it will work because you want it to work. This is called **Confirmation Bias.** *(See Appendix A for more details)*

₅ As time passes and you two become an item, you begin to witness those negative traits unravel. The mission is accomplished—you're attached. With attachment secured, there's no reason for the brain to seek further *attachment* traits. Instead, it starts seeking *detachment* traits; what goes up, must come down. Now, you discover the numerous negative attributes that were previously apparent but ignored or underestimated.

₆ **Attachment Theory** provides insight into how confirmation bias affects relationships. *(See Appendix B for more details)*

₇ With your detachment radar activated, you process things with the precision of an iMac. You realize this guy isn't such a great match after all, recognizing his unappealing habits. When you ask him to consider changing his ways, he views it as controlling. He insists it's not him who changed; you're just now seeing the real him. Oddly enough, you're convinced it's him who has changed, because this person standing before you now wasn't the one you knew before. In short, the relationship crumbles, and blame is tossed back and forth.

₈ **Why did you miss the red flags?** Mainly because when you're attracted to someone, you're excited about them. Your brain and body crave more of that, so it avoids anything to the contrary.

₉ To avoid the pitfalls of missing red flags, maintain a physical or *mental* list of traits and habits you dislike. Check these off your list as they arise in someone new. I know this sounds overly technical and tedious for a relationship, which is supposed to be built on love, but many successful people will tell you they've built their financial empires through planning—checking the dos and don'ts. Why should a relationship empire be any different?

₁₀ Remember, this can simply be a mental list, but first, you must compile it. What don't you like? What do you expect from your partner? What don't you expect from your partner? If you could create your perfect husband, would he frequent the same places as this guy? Would he have similar friends or wear similar clothes? Would he initiate contact as often as you do? Would he trust you alone in his room? Remember, this list should be reviewed before the relationship is formed, not 2 years in.

11 Sometimes, a handsome face and a great sense of humor can blind women to these questions. And if the sex is good, she can be blind for literal years.

Some common Red Flags include:
- Lack of communication
- Controlling behavior
- Trustworthiness issues
- Abusive or aggressive tendencies
- Irresponsibility
- Poor problem-solving skills
- Chronic procrastination
- Bad reputation
- Public flirtation
- Lack of self-sufficiency
- Resistance to personal growth

12 These are just a few warning signs to watch out for. No man is perfect, but there's someone who's a perfect fit for you. That ideal match may come with flaws, but their willingness to acknowledge and address their flaws will determine if they're worth your time.

13 While creating lists and monitoring the progression of your relationship, always prioritize *love over list*. Ultimately, love has the power to transform your outlook of someone. Have you ever initially disliked a particular look

or trait in a person, only to grow fond of it because someone you loved possessed it? True love can make you overlook your dislikes. However, if any of these dislikes are fundamentally detrimental to your way of life, they should be avoided at all costs.

₂ BAD MEN SELECTION

₁ Humans naturally seek comfort, ease, and familiarity. We prefer not to constantly look over our shoulders or live in a state of anxiety. Consequently, we gravitate towards situations we're accustomed to, as they feel safer and more predictable. However, this inclination often holds us back because unfamiliarity breeds a fear of change. Sticking to familiar paths feels more secure than venturing into unknown territory.

₂ The first person you deeply fall in love with often sets a template for future partners. You fall for certain traits rather than the individual themselves. You might find yourself saying, *"I like a guy who does/works/wears _____."* This tendency to connect the dots of familiarity leads you to associate a <u>new partner</u> with an <u>old flame</u>. But here's the catch—they're not the same person.

₃ I've observed women choosing one man's profession over another's, even when both offer identical benefits, income, and time off. They latch onto a particular job title because they've previously found success with a man who held that same title, failing to see that a job title is merely a label; It's the fruits of his labor that truly matter.

₄ This tendency applies to poor choices in partners, as women often repeat the same patterns without realizing it. Love and happiness are not defined by labels or job titles. You must remain open to any man who *meets your standards*, regardless of his profession.

₅ When you select men based on past experiences, your defenses are often lowered. This tendency is particularly prevalent among women who have previously been involved with abusive partners. They may overlook signs of aggression or control, sometimes even finding excitement in the drama and conflict. For them, love is synonymous with chaos, believing that his emotional reactions are proof of his love. This belief can drive them to provoke him further, seeking that intense, fiery response. Although others urge her to leave, she interprets his anger as a sign of love, making it difficult to break free.

₆ When she dates other men, she seeks the same passion that once excited her. Scarred by her first deep love, she mistakenly views composure and calmness during arguments as signs of indifference. An emotionally stable partner who manages conflicts maturely might seem weak or disinterested to her.

7 When choosing your next partner, it's crucial to keep an open mind. Don't restrict yourself to the qualities of your first true love—there was a reason that relationship didn't work out. Remember, the definition of insanity is doing the same thing over and over again and expecting a different result.

8 Understand that our brains seek comfort, and this preference for familiar traits will repeatedly draw you to similar men. Even if you believe he's different, it might just be his job title, clothing style, or skin tone that sets him apart. But ask yourself: *is his character truly different?* If the answer is *"no,"* then it's time to switch things up. If he *is* actually different, it may be your interactions with men that are the constant factor. In this case, to achieve a different result, you'll need to adopt a new approach in your relationships. Watch to see if you are handling with these men in the same manner.

₃ REEVALUATING YOUR STANDARDS

₁ There comes a time when you may question whether your standards are too high or too low. As life circumstances change, expectations that once seemed reasonable may now appear *unrealistic*, especially if you can't meet those same standards yourself. It might be necessary to reassess your criteria or take a break from dating until you can align with those expectations. For instance, demanding a partner who owns two houses when you don't own any might be an unreasonable stretch.

₂ However, be cautious when considering revising your standards just because you haven't found someone who meets them. This mindset *often* comes from <u>desperation</u> rather than genuine <u>evaluation</u>.

₃ But I believe that standards and expectations largely stem from our comfort zones—things we feel comfortable with. Our comfort zones are shaped by past experiences, upbringing, cultural background, and personal values. These factors influence what we perceive as acceptable or desirable in a partner. For instance, if you've always felt secure with someone who communicates frequently, you might set a standard that your partner should text or call you often. Similarly, if you've grown up valuing financial stability, you might expect your partner to have a steady job or own property.

₄ Comfort zones also dictate our reactions to different situations. When we encounter something outside of our comfort zone, such as a partner with a different communication style or lifestyle, it can feel challenging or unsettling. This discomfort often leads us to set standards that reinforce what we already know and feel safe with.

₅ However, it's important to recognize that while our comfort zones provide a sense of security, they can also limit our growth and potential for happiness. Rigid standards based solely on comfort can prevent us from exploring new experiences and forming meaningful connections with people who might differ from our usual type. Therefore, while it's *natural* to have standards and expectations, it's equally important to remain *open-minded* and adaptable, allowing room for personal growth and deeper, more fulfilling relationships.

₆ Here's another idea, before revising your standards, consider expanding your pool of potential partners. It may not be that your standards are too high or low but rather that you've limited your options. You might need to broaden your acceptance criteria to include a wider range of high-quality men.

₇ As I discussed in **LEXI 2:1**, don't restrict your choices based on labels. You might envision your *ideal* man as a

sales manager making 85k/year, but your true love could be a **yoga instructor who owns a thriving business that has potential to go from 65k/year to 85k/year**.

8 Your expectations from a man should be consistent with what you expect from yourself. A relationship is a partnership that should be equivalent in effort. Before a relationship is established, it is often expected that the man takes the lead in pursuing the woman. This dynamic aligns with traditional courting practices where the man initiates contact, plans dates, and generally makes the first moves to express his interest. This pursuit can create a foundation for a relationship by demonstrating his commitment and desire to invest time and effort.

9 However, it's important to recognize that this dynamic requires reciprocity. If you show no interest or are unwilling to engage in the conversations he initiates, you should not expect him to persist indefinitely. Genuine interest must be mutual. A relationship cannot be built on one-sided effort; both parties need to show they are interested and willing to invest in getting to know each other.

10 While some men might tolerate any treatment from a woman, perhaps out of a sense of obligation or low self-esteem, most worthwhile men—those who value themselves and seek a genuine connection—will not. They are likely to

move on if they feel their efforts are not reciprocated or appreciated. It's important to show interest if you want to build a meaningful relationship with a quality partner.

₁₁ If you are content being single and prefer to remain that way until someone makes an exceptionally strong case for changing your status, then this advice may not resonate with you. This perspective is more applicable to women who are actively seeking a relationship and want to create a connection with a partner who values mutual effort and respect.

To summarize:
1. **Natural Pursuit**: Traditionally, men are seen as the primary pursuers in the initial stages of a relationship.
2. **Reciprocity**: Show genuine interest if you want to maintain his interest; relationships require effort from both sides.
3. **Worthwhile Men**: Quality men will not tolerate being undervalued; they seek mutual respect and genuine interest.

Understanding these dynamics can help you navigate the early stages of dating more effectively.

₁₂ It may be wise to revise your core principles if it means personal growth for both you and your partner. Let's say you once insisted, *"I'll only date smokers because I smoke.* " If you find yourself falling for a non-smoker who encourages you to reconsider, that's a positive change—<u>embrace</u> your personal growth. Conversely, if you have a strict *no-smoking policy* and fall for a smoker who pressures you to start, revising your policy to accommodate him isn't wise. Smoking is hazardous, and adopting risky behaviors *isn't* growth; and we know the <u>opposite</u> of growth.

13 A man wants to feel masculine in his relationship. A woman of <u>standards</u> who holds him accountable will make him *feel* like a true man—*if he has one inside of him.* So, don't hesitate to correct him when his approach to life is fundamentally flawed. It's said that a man enjoys driving the car; but he doesn't appreciate being criticized for choosing a particular route. However, he doesn't mind if his woman asks, *"Is this the quickest route?"* followed by, *"I ask because..."* This approach works far better than, *"OMG, you're going the wrong way!"* The best way to challenge his <u>masculinity</u> is with your <u>femininity</u>. *(See Appendix C for more details)*

4 WHY LIVE A LIE?

1 The online dating era has made it so much easier for people to create personas for the public to see. We all share information about ourselves, some more than others. But through their conversation, someone can gather enough info to

create a blueprint of their likes and dislikes. Social media has made it easier for men to cater to a woman's wants and needs because they're usually laid out on her own timeline. So of course, he loves to travel and wants to visit Paris one day just like you do; you told him 9 months ago on a Facebook post to your mother. If he's truly into you and has made you his next target, he has no problem waiting and gathering information about you. It sounds creepy and sneaky, but often it's not even done purposely. It sometimes just comes with being on social media and having a crush on someone.

2 When a man can build the exact type of man you want, just to get his foot in the door with you, he probably will. But why would he build a man he can't live up to? Simply put, he believes once you get to know him, you will already have an attachment to him, making it hard to separate. He just needs to hold up his false persona long enough.

3 A key indicator that a man might be creating a false persona is if he tries to accelerate the relationship unusually quickly. He may be attempting to secure your attachment before revealing his true nature. The deeper your commitment, the sooner he feels he can abandon the facade.

4 He feels he has nothing to lose. Without creating a fake persona, he likely won't capture your interest. By fabricating a false image, he increases his chances of getting you, even

though he risks losing you later. In his mind, the lie can only improve his odds.

₅ When you eventually discover that he lied about who he was initially, there are two possible outcomes: either you leave him because the real him isn't what you want, or you stay because the real him isn't that bad and/or you have become emotionally attached.

₆ If his primary goal is just to have sex with you a few times and maybe go on a date or two, fast-tracking the relationship allows him to achieve those goals before his behavior change becomes apparent. In the end, living a lie can benefit him. At worst, he will lose a woman he could never have had anyway. This is why living the lie makes sense.

₅ WHAT VERSION OF HIM DO I PULL OUT?

₁ Most people try to be as water in a relationship. They try to be somewhat flexible for their partner and vice versa. Being that a relationship is a partnership, certain things are agreed upon that maybe their previous partner never gave a second thought to.

₂ Every woman has her own set of standards and expectations. For a man to be with you, he must meet your unique criteria, but your definition of perfection is subjective. Different women have different standards, which means a man might have to adjust his behavior accordingly. Thus, a man who was terrible in one relationship might be great in another because of differing expectations and tolerances.

₃ For instance, he may have been faithful in a previous relationship but cheated in yours, or vice versa. Each woman's distinct standards and boundaries can influence how he behaves. He acts according to what he perceives as acceptable within each individual relationship.

₄ Ultimately, this means that a man's behavior can vary significantly depending on his partner's expectations and what she is willing to tolerate. The success or failure of his actions largely depends on the specific dynamics of each unique relationship.

₅ It's kind of like the difference in certain jobs. This job may *allow* mobile phone use; another job may *prohibit* phones on the premises. If an employee has to use their phone regularly, the job that has a *no-phone policy* will have tons of issues with them and their phone use. The company that allows phones will have little or no issues with their constant phone use because they aren't breaking any rules.

₆ If you ask the *no-phone policy* company what type of worker that particular employee is, they may have some disparaging words in comparison to the *open-phone policy* company. The *view*s of the employee are different, but the employee is the same person on both jobs. Their *need* to use the phone had not changed regardless of whose time clock they were on. Neither company intentionally revealed a different person; rather, their own standards and expectations brought out different aspects of the same individual.

₇ So, while you may wonder which version of him you're pulling out, the difference might be due to your unique standards and expectations. Think about this, no one <u>technically</u> commits a crime until there are laws & regulations against that act.

₈ But to continue with the above scenario, if the *no-phone policy* job was important to the employee, they would undoubtedly change their phone habits. When you want something or someone to remain in your life, you make the necessary changes for it.

₉ Certain people give off certain vibrations. So naturally, certain women can give a man different energies. Depending on what these energies are, it can help push or pull a man in either direction. Being at peace with self can spill out into your relationship for a positive effect. Negativity can also dim your relationship under a dark cloud.

₁₀ The man that *you* pull out of him can actually just be the woman you see inside yourself; a mirror. Being self-aware of how you treat others is important, but being aware of your own vibrating state is more so. You can't fully control anyone, but you can give them your best. Always do your part. If they fumble that, they have to turn you over.

₆ HE REFUSES TO GET A LEGITIMATE JOB

₁ It may come a time when you question his drive and ambition. These are usually traits that you would pay close attention to before getting serious. But unfortunately, sometimes these things slip through the cracks. Or sometimes you believe you can change him - fix him up, upgrade him. Only to find out the hard way that he has to **want** this change for himself.

₂ When people only know one way of life, they tend to follow it until they are convinced, shown, and proven that a better way is possible for them. It becomes difficult to tell someone how to make their money when you can't simultaneously present a more appealing alternative.

₃ Some people are not fans of structure. They want to come and go as they please. Often guys who get their money from illegal activities enjoy the *freedom* of making their own schedule. Ironically enough, if they get caught it is their *freedom* that will be taken away. But these guys are usually more equipped to be self-employed versus your typical 9-to-5 workers. So the everyday job may not be appealing to him.

₄ If he's able to make it through life okay and everything seems to be going fine with his current lifestyle, he probably won't change it. Sometimes it takes a man losing something to wake him up - his freedom, his kids, a parent, his homeboy, his money, or his woman. But when you've been in *hell* all your life you tend to lose track of the fire.

₅ In order to inspire change in him, it's crucial to present a lifestyle that resonates with his current one. Identify his passions or interests and explore avenues to turn them into profitable ventures. You might need to craft a detailed business plan to vividly illustrate the potential.

₆ The key lies in encouraging him to invest his earnings into a well-conceived, legitimate business endeavor. He must visually grasp the opportunity rather than just hear about it.

₇ This situation serves as a critical test of his leadership and foresight. If he cannot envision a future that avoids the risk of separation from you and your family, it raises serious concerns about his ability to lead you through life's challenges. Effective leadership in a relationship involves not just guiding, but also listening and adapting.

₈ Imagine a scenario where a man is driving towards a brick wall. Despite his partner's clear warnings about the impending obstacle, he chooses to ignore them and continues on his path. This behavior indicates a lack of situational awareness, adaptability, and respect for his partner's input. A man who cannot heed warnings or consider alternative perspectives is setting himself—and potentially the relationship—up for failure.

₉ Leadership in a relationship is about collaboration and mutual respect. It requires the ability to listen, adapt, and make decisions that benefit both partners. If a man is unable to do this, it reflects poorly on his capacity to navigate the complexities of a committed relationship.

₁₀ Therefore, this test is not just about his ability to lead, but also about his willingness to work together towards a common vision. If he cannot demonstrate these qualities, it may be a sign that he is not ready to lead effectively in the relationship. Some men need to see a plan as plain as day, some don't. Either way…effort matters.

7 IS THERE LOVE AFTER HEARTBREAK?

1 The short answer is *yes*. What people often fail to realize is that love, happiness, and joy aren't exclusively tied to a person, place, or thing. They can be found anywhere and in any form. To assume that you will never *feel love* again is ridiculous. Will love come in the **exact** form you believe it should? Not necessarily, but very possibly. You can't get caught up on the form in which you receive your blessing if that blessing is fulfilling.

2 Women email me asking for the cure to finding new love and I tell them *the path is the road within*. I know, it sounds cliché and obnoxiously philosophical. But when you suffer from heartbreak, your vibration lowers. The music you select to listen to usually supports the lower vibration you're on. Your day-to-day conversation speaks to it as well.

3 Remaining on such a low plateau will only attract other vibes that are similar. Not many positive people want to be

around someone who's always down. So when I say that *the path is the road within,* I mean you have to work on *you.*

₄ When you can't find progress in relationships, the progress you find should be with yourself. *If you're not growing, you're dying.* A fundamental piece to growth is progress. If you can find ways to grow your mind, body, and spirit, you can raise your vibration and begin to attract the lovely things you're looking for.

₅ Accomplishments can make anyone feel better about themselves. People often turn to the gym for the first time after a breakup, why? Because when you begin to improve how you look on the outside, it makes you feel good on the inside. The idea of doing something you've been putting off for years is very gratifying. I always suggest that after heartbreak, women should turn to self-improvement activities. Turn to goals and aspirations you've been holding off from.

₆ Take the time you were spending with him and redirect that love and energy to something that will pay off. Use him as *fuel,* if need be, at least until you've fully come to closure with the situation.

- Maybe start your online business; find ways to make passive income.

- Change your scenery - travel more. Many underestimate how important a change of scenery can be.
- Go back to school for a few months and add to your education.

7 As you progress and grow, you will almost literally begin to stitch yourself back together. Understand that each goal line you cross is another stitch across your broken heart. So get active and use your free time wisely.

8 Once you have replenished and healed, your energy will radiate more brightly. The people you wish to attract will notice this elevated vibration. This is when you are truly ready to receive love. By investing time in self-love and valuing yourself, you create an aura that others can't help but recognize. If you feel worthless, that sentiment will likely be mirrored by those around you. *(See Appendix D for more details)*

9 When a relationship is formed, an exchange of love takes place. Let's say two glass cups filled with love get swapped between the two lovers. He has his cup, and you have yours. When your heart gets broken in the relationship, that glass cup of love you're holding shatters, and the love pours out. You no longer have your cup or your love.

10 At this point, should this broken person look for love? No. They first must fix the glass in order to be able to fill it up

again. This is where self-improvement, goal-crushing, and progress come in. Start by filling yourself with self-love, appreciation of your growth, and spiritual love through Christ or whichever higher source of divine energy you connect with. Then, let the love you found within pour into your renewed glass cup.

11 Remember moving forward, your heart has been broken before, making you sensitive and fearful of anything that might hint at danger. The more time you take to heal, the more confident you'll be when entering a new relationship. During this healing process, not only does your heart become whole again, but you also gain the assurance that you can be content on your own if necessary. You learn how to cope with heartbreak, which brings a new level of confidence and openness to letting love flow naturally through you. You become less dependent on someone else's love because you have an endless supply of love within yourself.

12 Each time you experience heartbreak and invest in self-care, you're also investing in your growth. Consequently, you find yourself achieving more of your goals along the way. I guess the saying, *"What doesn't kill you can only make you stronger,"* proves to be true once again.

Read Lexi's story again, what do you think the problem was?

"THE MAN THAT *YOU* PULL OUT OF HIM CAN ACTUALLY JUST BE THE WOMAN YOU SEE INSIDE YOURSELF; A MIRROR."

- MANUEL V. JOHNSON | LEXI 5:10

THE BOOK OF

COURTNEY

OUR RELATIONSHIP HAS LOST ITS FIRE

T he bedroom plunged into darkness the moment Courtney switched off the television. She shifted in bed, shielding her ears from the rhythmic snoring of her boyfriend, another night passing without intimacy. Doubts gnawed at her; was she the root of this disconnect? She thought. Although Malik seemed more open with his emotions, his physical interest in her appeared to dwindle.

After four years of deep love, it was the absence of passion that troubled Courtney most. The once bright spark in his eyes when he looked at her had dimmed to a mere flicker. She had changed her hairstyle three times this month alone, yet he hadn't noticed. Compliments were few, and any sweetness felt obligatory, lacking genuine warmth.

Sex had lost passion, feeling more like a chore than a shared pleasure. Most days, Malik showed no interest in intimacy. Even when they did make love, Courtney kept her shirt on, self-conscious about the slight weight gain around her waist. She began to blame herself, questioning if she was the cause of their diminishing connection. When she brought the subject to Malik, he brushed her concerns aside, dismissing any notion of trouble. In her heart, Courtney feared he might be seeing someone else.

₁ LOVE GAINED AND LUST LOST

Love: An intense feeling of deep affection.
Lust: Very intense sexual desire.

₁ Often, when a man meets a woman, his initial attraction is predominantly physical. Her jokes may seem funnier to him if he's physically attracted to her. This attraction can lead him to tolerate behaviors or characteristics he might otherwise find unacceptable, simply because of her stunning appearance. However, as time together progresses, the physical attraction may fade slightly, while his mental and emotional connection to her deepens.

₂ Forming an emotional connection can be challenging without a shared history, but it's easier with someone who has helped create cherished memories with you. This emphasizes that with time comes emotional growth, ushering in *love*. In this process, lust becomes less important as the stronger connection of love takes center stage.

₃ Relationships that begin with intense passion often undergo changes as the initial excitement diminishes over time. When a man's sexual passion is at its peak, and he is adventurous in the bedroom, he may see his partner primarily as a sexy, exciting companion with whom he feels a deep connection.

4 However, as the relationship evolves and your roles expand—you become the mother of his children, the person who handles household chores, and the one with whom he occasionally argues—your position in his life changes. You transition from being just a sexy partner to a more essential, multifaceted life partner. This evolution often leads to a deeper, more meaningful connection where love takes precedence over lust, resulting in a higher *love-to-lust* ratio.

5 He begins to view you less as a *lover* and more as a *mother* – like the person that helped raise him as a child. This may sound negative, but it's not necessarily so. This stage often precedes marriage if he truly loves you and isn't seeking a new lust connection with someone else. It doesn't guarantee marriage, but it's a stage well above simply lusting over you.

6 However, this is where it gets tricky. If he can no longer see you as a source of **lust** and only views you as a **love** connection, he may seek his lust fix outside the relationship. This often leads to cheating. While the initial spark of the *Infatuation Stage* may dwindle, the love connection continues to grow.

7 It's important to note that I'm referring to a growing love connection, not suggesting that his love for you has reached its peak. Love at its highest peak does not involve cheating. So, if you're wondering how a man can cheat on a

woman he loves, this might explain it. His love has not peaked, it's growing. But while it's climbing the mountain of emotion, at times its footing may slip.

8 Remember, love exists on different levels, with the highest form being where he wants what's best for you, even *if* it's to his own detriment; it is unconditional. This depth of love isn't achieved in a single defining moment but is an accumulation of the little things over time. Just as spending one long day in the gym doesn't make you an elite basketball player; love grows through various levels depending on how he treats you and nurtures the relationship.

9 So, while he may love you, his love may not be deep enough to prevent him from seeking a new *lust connection* instead of rekindling that connection with you.

10 This paradox can explain why, as the emotional bond between you strengthens, the passion in the bedroom may seem to diminish. For him to fill your cup with love, he must first empty his cup of lust, fill it with love, and then share that love with you. In the process of this exchange, you notice the desire and lust is removed from his cup. The closer you become, the more the relationship evolves from just mere passion to deep emotional *intimacy*.

₁₁ Intimacy in a relationship goes beyond physical attraction and includes *emotional, intellectual,* and *experiential* bonds, which are important for enhancing sexual intimacy.

- **Emotional** intimacy involves sharing feelings and experiences, building trust, and creating a sense of security. This deep emotional bond encourages vulnerability and openness, leading to more meaningful and passionate sexual experiences.
- **Intellectual** intimacy arises from stimulating conversations and shared ideas, building admiration and mental connections. This can translate into a deeper attraction and desire.
- **Experiential** intimacy is formed through shared activities and quality time, creating a sense of togetherness and partnership. These shared moments strengthen the emotional and physical bond.

₁₂ By nurturing emotional, intellectual, and experiential bonds, partners can deepen their overall relationship, leading to a more passionate and fulfilling sexual connection.

₁₃ Achieving a balance between love and lust is a delicate and ongoing challenge. But understand that lust is fleeting, a brief spark in a moment of intimacy, while true love is enduring, a flame that sustains through time. Most women can get his lust, but they can't always get his love.

2 HIS SEX DRIVE HAS DECLINED

1 Many factors can lead to his decreased sexual desire. Some of these reasons have nothing to do with you. As men age, their bodies go through different changes and stages. Naturally, as we grow older, our bodies understand that the time for prime reproductive capability is closing. We are no longer crucial for human reproduction. Our sexual senses that drive us to have sex and reproduce begin to diminish with age, which is why Viagra is more common among older men. This process is usually gradual, so while pills may not be necessary for your man, he may still be experiencing minor effects from this *diminishing* process.

2 Every man is different - some may never experience this issue, while others may take pills in private to save face.

1. **From ages 25 to 30, a man's testosterone levels begin to decrease naturally.**

3 At these young ages, the effects are minimal, but they decline moving forward. Testosterone, a steroid hormone,

promotes the development of male secondary sexual characteristics, which include increased muscle mass, a deeper voice, facial and body hair, broadening of the shoulders, enlargement of the Adam's apple, and increased bone density. It also fuels sex drive. Therefore, experiencing what doctors' call *"Low T"* can be likened to having a low gas tank for his sex drive.

2. Mental blocks like *Sexual Performance Anxiety* can kill his desire at any mention of sex.

4 Performance Anxiety, as it relates to sex, is nervousness experienced before or during sexual activity, typically affecting one's ability to have successful or satisfactory sex. This may seem far-fetched, but Sexual Performance Anxiety is more common than many people think. During a Sexual Performance Anxiety attack, the body releases powerful stress hormones such as epinephrine/adrenaline and norepinephrine. These hormones tighten and narrow blood vessels, reducing blood flow to parts of his body, including his penis. For him to achieve an erection, blood needs to flow.

Do you see the dilemma here?

5 Erectile Dysfunction can be caused by physiological or physical conditions. If he's not sharing this information with you, it may *seem* as though you are the cause of his erectile

difficulties. So, make sure not to be too hard on him, because not being able to get hard is hard enough. For most men, it is embarrassing and something they do not want to share, fearing judgment and the possibility of their partner seeking intimacy elsewhere. However, once a man accepts his condition, he may feel more comfortable sharing his experience with you.

3. **The mischievous side of his declining sex drive can be due to other sexual outlets. This can include *masturbation* or *another woman*.**

₆ I've had women ask me why their men masturbate so much. They have a bittersweet overall outlook on the topic. On one hand, they're happy their man chose to pleasure himself instead of sleeping with another woman. On the other hand, these women feel left out of their man's sexual activities. They feel as though they should be involved with their partner's sexual escapades.

₇ Masturbation also raises questions about his fantasies. Is your man fantasizing about other women while pleasuring himself? Does this mean he would be more open to sleeping with another woman sooner than a man who doesn't masturbate while in a relationship? Or does he masturbate while thinking of you? Have you given him plenty of new material to fantasize about, or is he using old videos

186 Know Thy Man

and pictures of women from before your relationship? Does his masturbation prevent him from cheating with these women? Or does it make him want them more?

8 According to a survey by *Illicit Encounters*, 700 out of 1400 men they polled stopped watching porn completely while having affairs.

9 Other research has found that people who watch porn and masturbate are less likely to cheat than those who don't. Nothing is 100% guaranteed, but I can tell you that when a man is horny and proceeds to masturbate to ejaculation, more often than not, he won't be in the mood to leave the house for a cheating session.

10 So, while his sex drive with you has declined because he is managing his urges via masturbation, this might be his way of satisfying desires that involve other women, with the intention of eventually suppressing his urges to cheat.

11 If his sex drive has declined due to sleeping with another woman, I don't think that needs much explaining. However, understand that cheating **isn't** the only possible cause for a diminished sex drive.

Simple steps to improve drive:

- Stop masturbating
- Drink enough water
- Eat healthier / Plenty proteins
- Get lots of sleep
- Stay away from stressful situations
- Exercise / Lift weights / Cardio

3 RELATIONSHIP HAS LOST ITS PASSION

1 We've discussed sex extensively, but many women find it difficult to maintain intimacy in their relationships. Intimacy is defined as a close, familiar, and usually affectionate or loving personal relationship with another person, characterized by a deep emotional connection, mutual trust, and a sense of closeness and understanding. It's a mouthful. Many refer to this bond when they express their oneness with someone. It's this attachment to someone that goes deeper than the surface.

2 At times, intimacy can involve a high level of physical affection and care. Not being able to keep your hands off each other is a form of intimacy in *action*. In fact, the *absence of sex* can be a test of intimacy - if there are high

levels of affection when sex is not an option, then intimacy thrives.

₃ When a relationship loses its spark, a variety of issues may be at play. Some of the previously mentioned factors could contribute to this unfortunate circumstance. While sex may still occur, it can become lackluster. It's important to remember that intimacy doesn't necessarily require sexual activity. Often, the real problem of losing passion can lie in the lack of trust, the repetitive daily routines, and predictable sexual encounters.

₄ Familiarity can sometimes lead to a lack of intimacy. When partners become too accustomed to each other, they may start taking each other for granted, leading to complacency and a decrease in effort to maintain closeness.

₅ **A FEW FACTORS THAT CAN HELP PROMOTE PASSION AGAIN ARE:**

- Resolve any trust issues that may have shaken your mutual trust. It's very difficult to look at your partner with passion if you are aware of lies they've told you.

- Spend time outside the house together. A change of scenery can help break the cycle of repetitive, robotic routines.

- Hold hands more often. Studies show that holding hands releases oxytocin, promoting bonding and a sense of togetherness crucial for intimacy.

- Give each other massages. Caressing your partner stirs up emotional responses and demonstrates care and compassion for their physical well-being.

- Share non-relationship-related fears. Intimate conversations about personal fears can lay the groundwork for physical intimacy through emotional understanding and empathy.
- Kiss different parts of the body unexpectedly. While a kiss on the lips is common, unexpected kisses on the forehead, chest, or inner forearm can evoke different emotions and invite intimacy.

- Begin sexual encounters from a different position each time. Starting sexual routines differently and keeping them fresh helps maintain excitement and break the monotony.

- Have sex in different places around the house. Changing locations, like the kitchen or living room, can bring a new level of excitement and create memorable experiences distinct from the bedroom.

6 Once strong connections are reestablished, trust between hearts rebuilt, and predictable sex sessions rearranged, intimacy can be reignited.

4 HE DOESN'T COMPLIMENT ME ANYMORE

1 Sadly, human beings have a habit of losing interest in things they once cherished. This applies not only to valuable items but also to people in our lives. When this happens in a relationship, women often question themselves immediately. You may question your appearance, your contributions to the relationship, or even your sexual appeal. Many times, you have no control over this situation. When someone's love for you is based on something superficial, it can easily be shattered.

2 When we first meet someone, their physical appearance often catches our eye, and our attraction to their looks is usually at its peak. On the other hand, we can also meet

people who weren't physically attractive to us initially, but as we get to *know* them, their personality and charisma create an attraction that not only heightens their physical appearance but goes beyond it.

3 When a man no longer finds his woman attractive, it sometimes reveals that his attraction to her was solely surface level. When a man genuinely grows attracted to his woman, he can find her endearing even when she *burps*. He might tease her for it, but her comfort with him, and her natural behavior can be attractive qualities. He may not compliment her on such behaviors, but they won't diminish his attraction. That's if their love has moved beyond superficial aspects.

4 I'm not suggesting you change your entire appearance based on a potential superficial outlook on his part. If he truly loves you, he should appreciate your new look just as much as your old one. His **love** for you shouldn't change just because your appearance has changed. His opinion of your appearance may change, but that's something you can discuss openly – his like or dislike for it.

5 I say all this to emphasize that if his love for you is deep-rooted, regardless of any changes in your appearance or behavior, his love for you should eventually lead him to love your new look because…. It's you.

₆ I remember when I first shaved my head completely bald; my significant other at the time didn't like it at all. She thought I looked sick. However, once she associated that bald head with the person she loved, her appreciation for bald heads grew.

₇ Keep in mind that this is all based on the premise that your appearance or actions have changed in some way.

₈ But to the topic of him not complimenting you anymore, a compliment is a kind gesture that can boost a person's confidence. Love is important, but acknowledgments and affirmations are equally as valuable. However, receiving the same compliment about the same thing every day isn't necessary either.

₉ No one wants to feel taken for granted; a compliment reassures your partner that you appreciate what they bring to the table. When we don't receive compliments from those we expect them from, we can feel unappreciated. But don't forget, their lack of attention to detail doesn't diminish your <u>worth</u>.

₁₀ Personally, I believe that if my woman wants me to grow my beard out, I automatically want to grow it out to please her. It makes me feel good knowing that she enjoys looking at me. On the contrary, if she loves beards and I can't grow one, I'll work on making her appreciate a smooth face along with everything else I offer.

₁₁ It's important to realize that no one we meet or are with is perfect. If someone leaves us because we gained a few extra pounds or due to our appearance, it shows their shallowness. I would argue that such a relationship lacked true love. If there was any love, it was only the most superficial kind.

₁₂ Give your partner reasons to be proud to be with you, and hopefully, they do the same for you. You know when you're at your best and when you're not, and your partner should see this too. If they don't, it speaks more about them than it does about you.

Read Courtney's story again, what do you think she should do?

"... LOVE ISN'T ACHIEVED IN A SINGLE DEFINING MOMENT BUT IS AN ACCUMULATION OF THE LITTLE THINGS OVER TIME"

- MANUEL V. JOHNSON | COURTNEY 1:8

THE BOOK OF

NESSA

ARE YOU GOING TO PAY FOR THIS

He slammed the front door in Nessa's face, and she refused to open it again. Their last words had been as venomous as the bite of an African black mamba, a fitting end to the worst argument they'd ever had. After these verbal clashes, Joseph always fled to his mother's house to unburden himself, ignoring Nessa's pleas for them to resolve their issue within their own home. To her fiancé, this never seemed to be an option.

196 Know Thy Man

Nessa thrived in her high-paying job at an advertising agency, while Joseph barely managed to make ends meet on his own. Despite their financial disparity, money had never been the foundation of their love. For Nessa, it wasn't about material possessions but about the emotional support that couldn't be bought—a kiss on the forehead and a listening ear were worth more than any new handbag.

Initially, their differing financial situations seemed manageable. But as their relationship deepened, so did Joseph's insecurities. He doubted his worth and questioned his ability to provide, which led to frequent arguments about money and gender roles within their relationship.

Nessa considered herself a traditionalist, yet her highly successful career often clashed with these values. She longed for a man who could be the breadwinner, but she always ended up footing the bill. She would have gladly submitted to a partner with the intelligence and ambition to lead their future family, yet she found herself mending the lives of grown men instead.

Despite Joseph's financial instability and lack of leadership, Nessa had focused on his looks and his undying love for her. While physical attraction and love are important, building a relationship solely on these factors proved insufficient for her.

Nessa grappled with the reality of wearing the pants in their home. Why did she keep attracting men who made her feel this way? As she stood by the closed door, she began to wonder if she was the problem.

₁ **MATERNAL PROTAGONISM**

₁ There's a term I created called *Maternal Protagonism* *(See Appendix E for more details)*. Some women possess a natural gift for giving and nurturing. Her having a childhood filled with love can lead to her showing an abundance of love to others as she grows up. Conversely, a lack of love during childhood can lead to a strong dislike for unloving situations, prompting these women to <u>demand nothing less than a generous outpouring of love.</u>

₂ Additionally, a <u>passion for parenting</u> and a desire to <u>maintain control of most situations</u> can also activate the Maternal Protagonist inside. Despite the varied causes, the outcomes remain consistent.

₃ The actions of a mother with her child are beautiful to witness, but when this nurturing extends to a man, things can get tricky. There's nothing wrong with giving love, especially when it's being reciprocated. But often these women overwhelm men with more love than they know how to handle. This can make the man feel babied, like a child, especially if he isn't prepared for such a role. He doesn't feel adequate to reciprocate her love, like how a child cannot fully reciprocate a mother's actions. The motherly energy can either attract or repel a man, depending on his position in life.

₄ If he has *Father Aura*, she may repel him. If he has *Son Aura*, she may attract him.

Father Aura is when a man exhibits a father-like presence with his woman. She should be regarded as his *equal* rather than his lesser. When expressed **negatively**, this energy manifests as excessive discipline without emotion. A man with Father Aura tends to be less receptive to emotions, making it difficult for a woman with *Maternal Protagonism* to connect with him. This aura can arise from either having an overbearing father or experiencing the absence of one during his childhood.

Son Aura, in contrast, represents a man's openness to receiving everything offered to him. He is like a blank canvas, ready for a woman to imprint her essence upon his foundation. This energy also stems from extreme maternal influences—either an abundance of love or a complete lack of it—leading to his deep yearning for affection. His capacity for love is typically reactive to the love he receives; when her affection wanes, so does his. Unlike Father Aura, Son Aura relies on external sources of love rather than being self-sustained.

₅ The ideal dynamic is for the woman to embody Sister Aura and the man to embody Brother Aura, symbolizing equality under the love of a parental figure. Their Mother and Father

Auras should be drawn from a higher source, whether that be religion or their shared goals and aspirations. This idea can be somewhat expressed in how The Bible considers us all **Children** *of God*. If we share a father, we are brother and sister. Achieving balance between these sibling auras is essential; if one possesses more than the other, conflicts arise. When both children are content, the entire family thrives under God.

₆ Now that we have a basic understanding of *Maternal Protagonism,* let's dive into the mindset of the type of men a woman with this trait will attract. Men with what I call *Nurturance Dependency Syndrome* (See Appendix F for more details). Many men seek women with these traits for various reasons. Typically, he is a man unprepared for the world, finding comfort in his woman's oversight, which acts as a pacifier for his problems. He might not be a businessman with a secretary, but his woman handles his financials and paperwork as if he needs one. Much like a mother would fill out her child's school enrollment forms, she takes the lead in his business affairs, which he loves.

₇ He avoids the day-to-day operations of life, relying on his woman to handle these affairs for him. This isn't because they agreed on a division of labor or because she is better at these tasks. It's merely because if she didn't do it, it wouldn't get done, even if it *solely* benefits him. Much like a mother completing a task her teenager ignored.

8 Men without drive and ambition are usually attracted to and become attached to women with *Maternal Protagonism*. Women who challenge him to improve and expect leadership or greatness make him uncomfortable. Unfortunately for him, a big part of growth and progression is being *uncomfortable* with the state that life is currently in. This is why being with these dead-end men can feel like a lack of progress in your life and in your relationship.

9 Women with *Maternal Protagonism* are sometimes attracted to a certain type of man for a couple reasons. Many people had their first child at a young age when they weren't fully prepared for parenthood - this might include you. These early parents may yearn for a second chance at parenting, to correct the mistakes they made with their first child. These mothers relish the opportunity to guide and improve someone's life, a trait that becomes central in their relationships. They find joy in helping mold the lives of their men into something greater. While some women might demand greatness from a partner, these women want to help build that greatness. This nurturing approach can be beneficial, but if this effort isn't reciprocated, it can become draining for her.

₁₀ Also a woman's attraction can sometimes stem from a fear of abandonment and a desire to control their significant other. The belief is that by controlling his way of life, he won't leave her like her father, mother, or a previous partner did.

₁₁ This fear fuels the woman's Maternal Protagonist role, and his acceptance of this dynamic acts as a crutch for her insecurities.

₁₂ For some women, the desire to help their partner is natural and commendable. However, it becomes problematic when this desire turns into an overbearing need for control, especially if her partner isn't receptive to it.

₂ ADDICTED TO FIXING MEN

₁ For many women, the act of *building* is inherently pleasing. Watching something come from nothing is a fundamental process we as a species can relate to. Some would say it's because our own existence spawned from the abyss of nothingness...and then there was light. As human beings, we love to create, and we typically honor those with the most creativity. The idea of constructing something with our touch almost makes us feel like gods. I raise this point to draw a parallel between the human instinct of improving our way of life and women who love to improve their man's way of life.

₂ As children, girls more than boys played house and had dolls that participated in imaginary marriages—the building blocks of her creative nature. Fast forward to adulthood, arts and crafts and home decorating become her new creative outlets. But in addition to those, her new man becomes her latest project. She starts by handling his legal fees, ensuring his child support is up to date, and helping him get his driver's license. She then goes shopping to update his wardrobe and buys him nice jewelry. She feeds him when he's hungry and makes love to him when he's horny. She congratulates herself for transforming a peasant into a king. But did she really?

₃ What has <u>he</u> done to make himself a king? What has he achieved to deserve these things from the world? He loves her, and she gave him everything, but she also loves him, and he's given her nothing. So why does his love get rewarded, but hers does not?

₄ Her problem is that she has crafted the outer shell of the man she desires, but the inner workings of a man she doesn't want. None of these efforts have changed his inner being. His mindset on life hasn't evolved because of her actions.

₅ Seventy percent of lottery winners go bankrupt. Why? Because to be a millionaire, you need ambition, common sense, resources, and knowledge. With these, all you need is the right business opportunity, and you may be on your way to your first million. But you also need those same skills to remain a millionaire. What it took to get your first million will be what it takes to keep your first million. Most lottery winners lose it all because they <u>never developed the skills</u> to earn their newfound riches. They never had the skills to be millionaires, and thus they played the lottery in hopes of skipping the line.

₆ This same equation applies to women turning peasants into overnight kings. He never developed the skills to be a king, so the chances of him disappointing her are much higher than she'd imagine. In her mind, she has shown him more love than any person can handle, so through loyalty alone, he should do right by her, right? Yes, that sounds good on paper, but the reality is, he's an old car with an old engine, sporting new tires and a custom paint job.

₇ So how *can a woman help* her partner build himself? Instead of identifying the problem, finding the tools to fix it, and then solving it for him, she should help him recognize the issue and guide him toward the tools—allowing him to fix it himself once he has what he needs.

Example:

- *Step 1*: Problem - Realize he needs a job.
- *Step 2*: Tools - Take Classes for trade school.
- *Step 3*: Fix 1 - Finish classes.
- *Step 4*: Fix 2 - Find a job.
- Step 5: Fix 3 - Perform well at the job.

8 Instead of his woman completing steps 1–4 and giving him the 5th, her involvement should be in step 1, allowing him to complete step 3 while merely giving him suggestions on steps 2 and 4. It's not her job to sign him up and set up his classes. It's not her job to take the classes for him because he's not as smart. It's not her job to find him a job, and it's not her job to make sure he keeps the job. As his woman, she is to assist him, not be his assistant; he isn't a CEO just yet. She is to help guide when he gets off track, not be his guardian who does the work *for* him.

9 You point him in the direction to get the tools that can build the house; you don't build the house for him. He won't respect it the same because he didn't build it. It's like how fast money is usually spent fast. People don't respect things as much when they know subconsciously that they didn't necessarily earn it.

10 Some of us have an eye for potential, and some of us believe we are so great that we can improve any situation.

Women, being natural creators, cultivators of life, and a little overconfident at times, walk into relationships believing in what *can be* instead of *what is*. They believe they are the ones who can turn this lump of coal into a pile of diamonds. They believe that whatever woman he was with before wasn't going to get the same result because she isn't the same woman. There's nothing wrong with that mindset, nothing wrong with believing in yourself. There *is* something wrong when you enter a red-flag situation, risking your heart because you believe you have what it takes to change him. Have you thought that maybe he doesn't want to change? You can be the perfect meal in the restaurant, but if he isn't hungry, he won't eat.

₃ FAILING WITH A LOSER

₁ Women often question themselves as to why they always end up with a loser for a boyfriend. One of the primary *reasons* can be attributed to her attention to his ***potential*** rather than his ***actual*** self. When you start dating someone for the first time, depending on your state of mind from the previous relationship, you may or may not notice his flaws. If you do notice them, they may seem fixable to you, especially if they are flaws that seem minor compared to the mishaps you encountered in your preceding relationship.

₂ You begin to make mental notes of these discoveries and save them for a later date. You have hope that once you two fall in love, all those minor blemishes can be fixed. As time goes on, you begin to conclude that he is either unwilling or incapable of making adjustments to improve his life. You find yourself trying to change the man instead of simply assisting the man. Depending on the guy, he may take offense to that. Imagine that… here you are trying to bless him with your fertilizer, and he's refusing to grow. At some point, anyone would get tired of watering dead grass.

₃ What happens quite regularly is that women often overlook his flaws and walk into the relationship blinded. I speak on the *Infatuation Stage* in **JASMINE 1:1**, where I touch on how a woman can be blinded in the beginning of a relationship.

₄ Now, if she falls in love before she notices his flaws, it can be tragic. Trying to *untie* two hearts that are eating each other alive can be strenuous. She then finds herself either working overtime to fix him, learning to live with him as he is, or packing her bags and accepting that she misjudged the situation.

₄ **WHO IS THE ALPHA FEMALE**

₁ As a leader, she may experience loneliness along her journey. You would think in a world of beta males, the alpha female could easily find a partner to mesh with her dominant spirit.

₂ It becomes difficult when the alpha female seeks an alpha male. And of course, she would seek the cream of the crop; it's what an *alpha* would do. That may easily work in business but may reveal itself to be challenging in an intimate relationship.

₃ The commanding personality and often described aggressive nature of the alpha female can scare men away. But keep in mind that every man who turns away from the alpha female isn't necessarily a beta. Some alpha males understand that an alpha female can cause friction. So at times, it becomes a question of being worth the effort. If an alpha male doesn't believe you're worth the effort, he may turn away. Every million-dollar business deal isn't a good fit for your business or brand. That applies here as well. The male lion understands risk-to-reward ratios and enters situations accordingly.

- The Alpha female may scare the Beta male due to insecurities regarding his position in her life.

4 The alpha female, through her actions, often pushes him to reflect on areas of his life he's lacking in. She challenges him; this forces the beta into an uncomfortable position. The alpha female naturally demands an alpha response, but when she has a beta male, the energy she receives isn't always satisfying.

5 She often doesn't show respect to the beta because she perceives his actions as weak through her alpha perspective. In many cases, she uses the beta for her benefit, seeing any gain he makes as merely the opportunity she has provided him. This may seem narcissistic, but it's important to note that these feelings don't apply to every man, just to those she considers low-level betas.

ALPHA FEMALE WITH HER BETA MALE

1. There are beta males that will mesh with her just fine, but 51% of that is dependent upon the alpha female.

6 She needs to reach a point in her life where she can recognize his value and understand the benefits he brings to her. If she genuinely wants the relationship to work, she must be patient with him.

7 Understand that his approach to life isn't driven by the same emotions as hers. What motivates her in the morning isn't the same for him. Her drive may not match his, but if

his motivation is sufficient to accomplish *his* goals, he feels successful.

8 She must understand and accept that happiness is what truly matters, not the societal goals imposed on us. Is he happy? If the answer is yes, there's no need to diminish that, especially if his happiness positively influences her as well.

9 A key point is to also make sure he isn't derailing her from her mission but instead encouraging her. She must be cautious that her beta male is capable of living vicariously through her. When he visualizes her success, he can see it as his success.

10 At some point, she may confront her true instinct, which doesn't include being content with life. However, not every beta male is simply satisfied with his current situation. Some want improvement as well.

11 When with *a beta male who seeks more from life*, a little nudge can be helpful. Fortunately, the alpha female is well-suited for this role. She will spring into action to support her partner, seeing him not as lesser, but as someone needing guidance. If he is eager for more and capable of learning, he will benefit from the direction provided by his alpha female. She uses her skills effortlessly to help him grow.

12 If she's an entrepreneur alpha, she may apply those same building skills to her man. The same way she grows a business and cultivates a brand, she approaches her relationships the same way. Taking an idea or a potential opportunity and turning it into her own pet project. More than not, she isn't doing it solely for him; it's a pleasure for her as well.

BETA MALE WITH HIS ALPHA FEMALE
2. *The other 49% of the equation is on the beta male.*

13 He must understand his role in the alpha female's life. He needs to appreciate her busy work schedule and her need for growth—mentally, spiritually, and financially. He must learn how to support her self-care efforts and be helpful, not jealous. He should be a voice of reason and calm, aware that her hectic lifestyle can create a hectic household. He must be her balance—the solid foundation she can rely on while conquering the world.

14 He also needs to ensure that his own life isn't stagnant. Leveraging his alpha female's strengths can be beneficial for his personal success as well. An alpha female loves growth, so seeing her significant other grow alongside her is a beautiful experience.

15 Her resources and knowledge are also his, as are the benefits of her drive and determination. While the beta may be

creative and okay with his current situation, the alpha female can often draw out skills, abilities, and artistry he never knew he possessed. It is in his best interest to embrace her alpha energy, allowing it to inspire him rather than shying away from it or feeling dominated by it.

ALPHA ON ALPHA

3. *The alpha female and alpha male often clash heads, but when it works, it's magic.*

16 Some of the most notable *alpha-on-alpha* relationships are with celebrities. Hollywood divorce rates are seemingly higher, and there are a lot of factors as to why, but I'll briefly share a couple with you.

17 One being that the partner they often choose is solely for self-reflecting status. Their interest is piqued by one's status in comparison to theirs, meaning they only wanted that person because that person's celebrity was equivalent to their own.

18 Probably the biggest cause of divorce in the entertainment business is due to time. When an empire has been built without someone else in mind, and their number one focus is to better their talents and accumulate more money, love usually doesn't have a place in that equation.

₁₉ Lastly, I'll say opportunities. In their space, they are awarded more opportunities to date other celebrities, so losing one isn't the end of the world. They believe in bouncing back, just as they have within their own careers. See, when you've sacrificed and lost so much as most celebrities have, you begin to believe you can make it through the most turbulent times. But the ego is inflamed, and pride often causes them to let go instead of humbling themselves to work things out.

₂₀ In order for the *alpha-on-alpha* dilemma to unfold properly, a true loss of ego must take place. Understand that the *bigger picture* is bigger than either of you individually; primarily because the picture should encompass *both* of you evenly. If you truly want to be with this person, you must be balanced. You have to stay within your feminine energy and he in his masculine. Feminine doesn't mean you're somehow submissive to every want and wish he has.

₂₁ Many have given femininity a stigma of being weak, but this is not true. The feminine acts as his twin in value, but not his twin in nature. They both, masculine and feminine, possess strength. The way they demonstrate said strength differs at times.

₂₂ Basic feminine traits *traditionally* are tenderness, cooperativeness, gentleness, empathy, affection, helpfulness, and demurity, just to name a few. While all these are true and are all positive characteristics, an alpha female also has the ability to turn these traits on and off when necessary, in relation to her environment. Depending on where she is and who she's around, she can fit her surroundings. And that is what makes the feminine so special—its fluidness. The capability of adjusting through situations seemingly effortlessly.

23 Timing is a key element of the feminine. Knowing when it's time to nurture and when it's time to attack. Our ancestors learned a lot about themselves through observation of wildlife animals. Take for instance, the lioness; she is the hunter of the pack—in essence, she prepares the dinner for the family. But watching her and her ladies collect the meal is such a feminine action. Although it may be perceived as masculine behavior to kill another animal, her purpose isn't murder for pure sport; it's for nourishment. So while she may seem to be in her masculine, she's still within her feminine guidelines.

24 While you remain in your feminine frame, he must remain in his masculine. If he wavers from this, the alpha female will take notice. A true alpha male knows this and will hold his stance firm. This defiant strength is what attracts the alpha female who is seeking an alpha male. She loves the lion's roar because his brute strength allows her to be in her

non-aggressive existence. This is why many women are attracted to men they feel have a bit of dangerous edge to them; they're allowed to be the total opposite on the spectrum. She believes that he can protect her not only from physical harm but also from emotional attacks, mental stress, financial strain, and a variety of other challenges.

₂₅ So we established that the alpha male's masculinity must remain intact. But, he must use his secret weapon that isn't usually associated with masculinity—that weapon is empathy. His leadership position depends on being able to read, understand, and communicate someone else's pain and sorrow.

₂₆ He cannot lead a household if he cannot read the room. His woman will need to know she has a backbone behind her. The best way to illustrate this is by showing her he understands and sympathizes with her outlook. He must include her in the journey as a co-pilot and not a passenger. A beta female wouldn't mind being a passenger, but an alpha female might need some time to adjust to that role.

₂₇ One of the biggest *alpha-on-alpha* problems is submitting. Yes, the evil word that's like garlic to the alpha's vampire ways. Here's what I've learned about submitting: when you submit to a <u>person</u>, you become their property in a sense. But when you submit to <u>love,</u> no one owns you at all. People think that when you submit, you submit to that *person*; on the contrary. When you submit, you're supposed to be submitting to the *love* that is shared between you two. You become *tied* to that love, and he does the same.

28 Your actions are always for the benefit of your love bond, which in turn benefits you and him equally. You act to build the love by doing the things you love for him. But at times, you also must sacrifice the things you have affection for if doing so builds the love bond as well—but *only* if it builds the love bond between you two.

29 When alphas can grasp this concept, they can allow their reluctance to go away and submit without obstruction. **Submitting isn't giving up yourself, it's pouring into your love.** Pouring your love into a pot together and trusting that neither of you will remove it.

30 Sacrificing something you want for the love between you and him may sound counterintuitive, and you may feel your partner should *just understand*, but sacrifice doesn't necessarily mean forever. Compromise is always an option that can be communicated. What you take away doesn't always have to stay gone. Sacrifice is merely an act of giving up something of value for something else deemed more important or more deserving at the time. So you have to self-reflect and determine if what you want is worth more

than what you've built with him. Ask yourself which brings you more happiness, which has made you a better person—him or the thing in question of sacrifice.

31 A serious sacrifice isn't something you will always be faced with in a relationship, but if and when you do, remember you aren't giving it up for *him*; you're giving it up for the *love bond* you've built.

5 THE BREAD WINNERS

1 Being the primary financial contributor comes with pressures that those in that role must constantly manage. Expectations and responsibilities are heightened when your performance in the world determines how others live under your roof. But along with those perceived added stresses comes a sense of pride and importance.

2 When it comes to women bringing home the bacon, you must be careful not to become as a parent to a child. Money should never define whose love is greater. If that were true, we'd all agree that millionaires love more in a relationship than the middle-class worker. We don't believe that, and it's because we know that love isn't the amount of money, but instead the action taken with the *available* money.

3 **Let's put this to the test:**

Name: Byron
Salary: $1.5 million/year
Gift: New Purse - $9,000

Name: Shawn
Salary: $45,000/year
Gift: Car Repair - $4,000

Is one gift greater than the other? Is the better gift the most expensive one solely because of its price? Only the recipients of the gifts can determine their importance. My only point is that price doesn't define whose love is greater.

4 I raise this notion because I want men and women to understand that being in a better financial position than your partner doesn't give you a pass on love. It doesn't mean you can throw money at your significant other and expect problems to disappear.

5 Usually, in a relationship, one person will make more than the other; it's rare they make the **exact** same amount. Often, it's pretty close, but when a couple's financial contributions aren't anywhere near the same, an understanding of what financial responsibilities and expectations will be required from both parties is essential. Will one pay all the bills,

while the other pays for activities like movies, dinners, and nights out? Will they split everything? Will one pay for dinner and the other leaves the tip? A relationship is a team, and I don't believe any team just hits the field and figures it out mid-play. You live with this person; you're building with this person, so understanding their habits is important. Laying your financial ideologies on the table is best.

6 Sometimes, even without a conversation, an understanding naturally develops between two people. This can happen after some time of living with one another. You kind of just learn their spending habits, and you make adjustments accordingly. The problem is that when they change their initial habits, and they've never <u>verbally committed</u> to their initial habits, you can't hold them to those habits. You can hold them accountable for their words about their habits, but you can't hold them accountable for your personal interpretation of their habits.

7 If they paid the internet bill the last two months and you two never discussed this setup, don't assume they will pay it this month. They may, but they may not. Especially in situations where they are moving into your house, rather than a home you both acquired together.

8 My point in saying all this is that communication is highly recommended because every relationship will function

differently. Being a breadwinner doesn't place you any higher in the relationship. This would explain why, in divorces, the financials are often split down the middle. It is widely recognized that **partners** build empires. The extent of each partner's contribution varies on a case-by-case basis.

₆ FINANCIALLY INSECURE MEN

₁ In today's world, more and more women are becoming the financial leaders in homes across free nations. As a result, many men find themselves in situations where their woman is ultimately responsible for their way of living. Some men embrace this, while others are embarrassed by it.

1. The man who embraces this lifestyle envisions himself as the recipient and his woman as the provider.

    He believes that his contributions in other areas, such as in the bedroom, offering moral support, or providing intimate care, compensate for his financial shortcomings. This perspective allows him to comfortably accept her role as the breadwinner.

₂ Women who find themselves happy in these situations usually *seek* support through other means, such as comfort during her stressful weeks, relaxation and relief in the bedroom, or someone who ultimately cares for her day-to-day well-being which can allow her to thrive in her element. Both parties in this situation accept the benefits, as they bring something different to the table.

2. When you have a man who accepts this role of being the recipient, *but* his woman's main objective is to have a man who can match her financial contribution, it can result in conflict between the two.

   Here, you have a woman who is with someone who cannot or has not given her what she feels she needs.

3 One may ask, *"What would cause a woman to remain or even get into a situation like this, knowing he wasn't what she was looking for?"* Several reasons can be named; one being that she wasn't who she is now. Sometimes we forge relationships at one point in life and later find that we grew into another stage without our partner. Innocently, we can grow financially through a new business venture, a raise at work, or a side hustle that took off. These are honest growths that are often *planned* but sometimes *unplanned.*

4 So ultimately, financial growth doesn't necessarily indicate they aren't aligned; it could simply mean she landed a job opportunity that he didn't. This financial opportunity places her at a pay grade he is not at. This means the

emotions attached to their relationship have not changed, re-sulting in a continuation of the relationship even though she in time may internally desire someone on her pay level.

₅ A more serious growth without our partner, which is not finance-related, is **mental** or **spiritual** growth. These growths on the contrary show a lack of connection between him and her. If they are truly *'one,'* how can one grow with-out the other unless they are on different pages? This is fine if you're willing to allow time for your partner's growth. The beauty of these two growths is that they often lead to finan-cial growth as well. Some say the lack of these growths is why many never grow financially - interesting to say the least.

3. When a woman accepts her role as the breadwinner, but her male counterpart isn't happy with his position, it can either motivate him or cause him to birth finan-cial insecurities.

₆ Being financially insecure isn't solely based on the actual money itself. It's more about his belief in where his self-worth stands. Not feeling he can provide for his family can bring great anxiety and depression. If you are the breadwin-ner, you may see no issues in the dynamic of the relation-ship. But if he cannot find his self-worth within his life and in your relationship, he may become a bit of an irritant to your financial growth.

7 Often, financially handicapped men who are traditionalists find themselves dealing with these feelings. Primarily because all their lives they were led to believe men are to be breadwinners and providers. While many women also agree, some don't carry stock in this relationship dynamic.

8 These traditional men doubt their worth, question their manhood, and often sabotage their own relationships. They strongly believe they need to *figure it out* before they are ready for a relationship. These men haven't grasped the idea that *financial* isn't the only way to show importance in a relationship.

9 If paying all the bills is something a traditionalist man believes a man should do, not being able to do so can drive him insane. And if he can't figure out how to *get to the bag*, he may figure out how to end the relationship.

10 A financially insecure man needs to know that without him, the house will not be able to function, but only if he is actually bringing something important to the table. There's no need to lie to him just to make him feel good. If he provides in other ways than financially, he needs to hear about it. Encourage him to reach his financial goals, but also

assure him he is needed, wanted, and still respected for what he does supply. But if he gives nothing, he should receive nothing.

Read Nessa's story again, what do you think she should do?

"SUBMITTING ISN'T GIVING UP YOURSELF, IT'S POURING INTO YOUR LOVE."

- MANUEL V. JOHNSON | NESSA 4:29

THE BOOK OF

BRANDY

HE'S JUST GOING THROUGH A TOUGH TIME

Operator: "Is he still in the room?"

Brandy: "No. Wait, I just heard his car start."

Operator: "Okay, stay on the line with me until officers arrive."

Brandy: "...okay."

As she held her phone shakily to her ear, Brandy glanced down at the broken glass scattered over their wedding photo. Tonight marked the end of their eight-year marriage. Like many women, Brandy had fallen for the traditional fairytale—growing up, finding Prince Charming, buying a house, starting a family, getting a dog... maybe even a goldfish. For years, Brandy had the life most women dream of. Mason, Brandy's husband, had a gift for selling products. He made millions reviving the inventories of failing companies. Their wealth was enviable, and he had proposed to a woman in Brandy who was eager to support and love her man through it all. His words of affirmation and affection had once kept their relationship strong.

But Mason's career took a turn when companies started adopting A.I. technology to cut costs, making creators like Mason obsolete. Financial issues led him down a dark path of depression. To cope with his perceived failures, Mason began drinking heavily, and soon became verbally abusive.

Staying out late, skipping showers and speaking in pessimistic terms had become Mason's new routine. Brandy did everything she could to encourage him, to rebuild the great man she had married, but nothing worked. The man who once uplifted her now drained her. His weekly jabs at her weight and the negative energy he brought into their home were tearing their lives apart.

Feeling hopeless, Brandy contemplated having the tough conversation—divorce. Mason refused to discuss it. She wondered if there was anything she could do to save their relationship. She knew he was supposed to lead, but that didn't mean she should stand by and do nothing while he battled his demons. Questioning her own loyalty, she wondered if she should stay by his side or leave before he broke more than just glass and picture frames.

Operator: "Units should be arriving now. Do you see them outside?"

Brandy: "Yes, I do. Thank you so much!"

₁ THE SAD MAN

₁ Depression for some feels like being alone in a stadium full of people. You can be surrounded by loved ones and still feel utterly isolated. This is why many turn to a higher power, something greater than themselves, to find peace in the present moment. Too often people become trapped in their own minds, unable to escape.

₂ Sometimes, the only perceived way out is through a bottle of liquor. What appears as destructive addiction to others may be seen as a release, a brief sense of freedom and peace. For some, the only way to liberate their minds is to harm their bodies, whether slowly or swiftly.

₃ Various triggers can plunge someone into this state: losing a loved one, a financial setback, betrayal by a trusted friend, or simply a buildup of perceived failures. Note the word *"perceived."* What one person sees as failure, another might see as stepping stones toward a larger goal. *A failure is merely an indication that the goal has not yet been achieved.*

₄ A man might encounter depression when he compares his current life to the life he envisioned for himself at this age, realizing he's far behind the eight ball.

₅ How do you help a man trapped in a constant dark rain cloud? First, understand that you will inevitably get wet, but you must move at his pace towards recovery. He's fighting a war in his head. Remember, don't take it personally. Although his reactions may seem directed at you, they aren't necessarily meant for you.

₆ However, if his reactions become abusive in nature, impacting you and your children negatively, you must prioritize their well-being. Often, *this* decision benefits your mental health as well.

₇ When helping someone with depression, don't expect anything in return. They may not acknowledge your efforts or offer thanks. Trust that what you're doing is saving their life, and when they emerge from their darkness, they will thank you. Until then, don't **expect** gratitude.

₈ Understand that money, sex, comedy, and adventures are unlikely to lift them out of their funk. What they need is time. Their brain needs time to process whatever is troubling them.

₉ Never impose a timeframe for their recovery. If you truly want to help, be there for them. Assure them that you will always be there and live that truth by standing by their side at every turn. Let them know that while there's nothing physical you can give to make them feel better, you offer your time and unconditional love. Offer them your life— metaphorically, not literally. Your job is to ensure they aren't fighting alone. Strongly reassure them they are not a burden because of the love you have for them.

10 A positive text message every morning can help show them you're there every step of the way. But remember; do not **expect** a reply or acknowledgment. The effects of your actions will be evident in the final results.

11 Amidst the noise of the world, a lonely soul can still echo; be the silent strength that steadies without seeking acknowledgment.

Symptoms of Depression:
1. Reduction in or loss of pleasure in activities
2. Excessive sleep or lack of sleep
3. Indecisiveness or problems with concentration
4. Agitation
5. Fatigue or loss of energy
6. Guilt or feelings of worthlessness
7. Suicidal thoughts, plans, and/or attempts
8. Major changes in weight or appetite

2 HIS LOW SELF-ESTEEM

1 A man's superpower often lies in his supreme confidence. When that confidence wanes, it can be a sad and unfortunate sight. Most men want to feel respected, capable, and powerful. When stripped of these three things, simply loving him might not be enough. Being unaware of this can lead to confusion in your relationship.

2 Many men have been conditioned by society to have low self-esteem. They let social media and television define what success and happiness look like. Ultimately, only they can define their happiness and measure their success. Remind him of this.

3 You might find yourself showering him with love and attention, yet your words could be cutting him deeply and challenging his sense of respect. Whispering his successes but shouting his failures is a recipe for low self-esteem. Be mindful of your words with a man who's fallen from his throne. A displaced man can be dangerous. When he's down on himself, ensure you're not adding fuel to the fire by affirming his perceived inadequacies. Worst thing you can do confirm his feelings of not being good enough. Even when he seems happy and back to normal, let him savor those moments and build on them. If he appears to be spiraling downward, remind him of his capabilities. Assure

him he just needs more time to figure things out, and <u>let him know</u> <u>you'll be there every step of the way</u>.

4 A non-judgmental partner is what most men need. The societal pressures of leading a family can be taxing, especially when one's gender is often defined by this role. While women are typically judged by how well they nurture, men are judged by how well they lead. Although, in today's world, these traditional roles are evolving.

3 **NEGATIVE ENERGY**

1 Sometimes a man's presence is so negative that you get a stomachache when he comes around, or you sense a dark cloud when he's near, just a heaviness in the air. This causes you to have unpleasant experiences when you're around him, preventing you from being truly happy in his presence.

2 Everything in the universe is composed of energy, which vibrates at different frequencies. Negative energy is someone vibrating at a low frequency. Imagine levels of frequency as literal numbered levels.

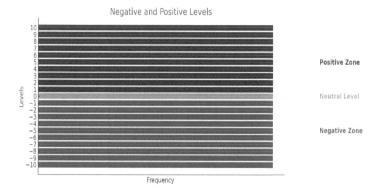

₃ Your basic frequency level of *being* is Level 0. Anything below that is in the negative zone. By visualizing it this way, we can see that negative energy can range from Level -infinity to infinity. Two people can be operating from negative spaces but at different negative levels; ultimately feeling like two different energies which will manifest as two different reactions. You want to cuss them out and they want to set your house on fire. Two negative energies, but one has clearly allowed themselves to slip further down than the other.

₄ The same applies to the positive side. You might be on a positive vibe but not vibrating as high as someone else. This can explain why you may think you and another person are perfect for each other, but it never materializes into a relationship. Although you two are vibrating positively, you aren't on the same positive frequency. For things to align properly, they must vibrate on the same frequency in some aspect of life. This means that every person you've ever

236 Know Thy Man

connected with matched your frequency in some form for some length of time.

₅ Knowing this, you should be more self-aware of the people you interact with comfortably. This should show you whether you're vibrating in the negative or positive zone, the key word is *"comfortably."* If you feel at peace while interacting with someone, you're in matched energy with them in that moment. But if you feel uncomfortable, you two aren't operating on the same level. The worse you feel, the further apart those levels are. You know the sayings, *"Show me your friends, and I'll show you your future,"* or *"Birds of a feather flock together."* The people you interact with reflect you at points in your current life.

₆ Have you ever had someone become so upset with you that they wanted to engage in a heated debate and grew even more irritated when you wouldn't engage? By not lowering yourself to their frequency level, you refused to operate in the same negative space where they wanted to release their negative energy. While they thought their yelling and antics were a display of strength and control, they were actually spiraling downward on the energy chart.

₇ Conversely, have you ever heard something positive or heard someone sound *"too happy"* in a video and your first thought/reaction was something negative? That's because in that moment you were functioning on a negative level.

8 This is important to monitor because being more self-aware is the steppingstone to true self-care.

9 Understand that when you vibrate at a negative frequency, you attract more negative energy because that's the level you're walking on. This blocks your blessings because certain gifts are ready to be given to you, but you need to elevate to the level where they reside. So always take the positive path; choose the positive choice.

10 The Christian faith encourages us to be more Christ-like for a reason. Christ is believed to have vibrated at the highest level of positivity, receiving every gift God had to offer. He turned the other cheek in the face of screaming mobs and rock-wielding men, maintaining his high vibration.

11 Pay close attention to your frequency, as the higher you vibrate, the more blessings you attract from *your* Creator. However, remember that while there are also gifts on the negative levels, those do not come from God. So, you may seem to be elevating, but the question is: by whom?

12 One way to identify if your man is too deeply immersed in negative energy is to pay attention to your body's reactions. If you feel sick in his presence, it could be a sign he's too far gone. The energy around you vibrates at a frequency that's not aligned with yours; your body will tell you. Have you ever been out somewhere, perhaps at a party, and felt like something bad was about to happen? The frequency of the people there didn't match yours at that moment.

13 Never be afraid to address your man's vibration—it might just save his life. A healthy relationship involves checking each other's frequency and keeping each other balanced. Once you address the energy he's giving off, show him the exact points where this negative energy is manifesting. Explain that your advice is meant to bring harmony to your relationship. Too many people are not harmonically balanced, living on different planes of frequency but staying together for sex, fear of societal judgment, or fear of their partner finding someone better. These reasons are understandable, but what's not understandable is how two people can remain together without putting effort into achieving peace and harmony.

14 Arguments and disagreements will happen, but having the serenity to solve these issues is crucial. Simply *hoping* someone changes is not proactive enough for a healthy relationship.

4 **HEALING HIS ANXIETY**

1 *How does one heal their anxiety?* They don't.
Their anxiety heals them. I believe our anxieties are chisels, tools placed upon us to shape us into beautiful sculptures of collected cosmic energy. These tools push us in life when we're stagnant. To understand this, you must accept that our troubles build our character. You might have heard the saying, *"What doesn't kill you can only make you stronger."* If life is perfect, why change it? We can't stay the same; we are growing beings. Everything *grows, dies, or never lived.* To grow, we need conflict. For your life story to unfold there must be *a story.*

2 <u>Embracing anxiety</u> is how you strip it of its power. When you fear it, you fuel it.

3 Your man may be experiencing anxiety, leading to sadness that dampens the relationship, causing issues in the bedroom, and more. Only his acceptance of his anxiety can help it lessen over time.

4 In 2015, I experienced my first anxiety attack. It happened months after I quit smoking and ended a previous relationship, and just weeks after releasing my first book, ***"The Mind of a Jerk | Diary of a Single Man."*** Imagine my surprise when the life improvements I thought I was making

turned into the worst year of my life. It wasn't until I identified and accepted my anxiety that things started to change. I even gave it a name (which I will not share, lol) and I started talking to it. When I felt an anxiety attack coming, I'd laugh and say, *"Come on in, bro. Do whatever you have to do, and let's get this over with."* By embracing it, the anxiety became just an annoying friend rather than a terrifying feeling of panic. Facing it with love instead of fear helped me tremendously. Over time, the anxiety attacks lessened, their intensity decreased, and they occurred less frequently.

5 As I closed the first half of 2015, I told myself, "So far, this is one of the worst years of my life." After the first six months of hell, I decided to turn the rest of the year into a blessing. I wrote two of my four books that year: *"In Love with a Stranger | Diary of a Married Woman"* and *"Last Words to a Dying Heart."* I wanted to take control of my life again...and I did.

6 When dealing with a man who suffers from anxiety attacks, remind him that embracing it takes its power away. He can't let it ruin his year; he must take back control. Let him know that no one has ever died from an anxiety attack, so he should let it flow through him. Encourage him to focus on his health: food, stress levels, and exercise. These will provide tangible points of good health and positivity.

Remind him of the chisel and how strong and beautiful he will be once the anxiety subsides.

5 THE LOST MAN

1 When a man loses his purpose, he loses his mind. He can also become unbearable to live with. You must ensure you don't lose your mind along with him. Negative energy can drag you down. When he's in a negative funk, it almost forces you to become positively stronger to deal with him. In a way, it's chiseling you both.

2 If you see him refusing to put forth any effort and your life is spiraling out of control as a result, a change might be needed. Some time away from each other may be helpful. Place yourself in more positive atmospheres. Let him know that if you stay, you won't have any positive energy left to pour into him. And if you have kids, someone has to have the proper energy to nurture them.

3 For a man who is **deeply lost**, a belief in a higher power must take him by the hand and lift him from those lower levels. He just simply needs to have <u>faith</u>.

Read Brandy's story again, is there anything they could have tried before they got to this point?

"EMBRACING ANXIETY IS HOW YOU STRIP IT OF ITS POWER. WHEN YOU FEAR IT, YOU FUEL IT."

- MANUEL V. JOHNSON | BRANDY 4:2

THE BOOK OF

ASHLEY

HE DID IT BECAUSE HE LOVES ME

S taring into the bathroom mirror, Ashley examined her bruises. The blood smeared across her lips felt both foreign and familiar. With trembling fingertips, she lightly traced the swollen eyes Jonathan had left her with. This wasn't the first time he had laid hands on her, and she feared it wouldn't be the last. She knew this feeling all too well, often dismissing these brutal moments as mere misunderstandings. Sometimes, she even blamed herself, concocting excuses to defend him. *"He grew up in a violent home." "I provoked him." "He's just possessive because he loves me so much."* Ashley viewed Jonathan's abusive behavior as *their* problem, not just *his*. They skillfully avoided questions, hiding the truth beneath layers of makeup. She saw them as one; his issues were hers. She believed in taking the good with the bad, thinking no one was perfect.

His abuse didn't start with his fists; it began with his words. The mental manipulation and degrading comments bled into her public life. Teasing her about her weight gain, constantly questioning her intelligence—these eroded her peace of mind, weakening her confidence and strengthening his control.

Her close friends would say, *"Ashley, we can see your bruises. We hear how he talks to you. Why won't you leave him?"* She never had an answer. Her response was always to downplay the situation. To Ashley, love was complicated and a concept her friends couldn't understand. So, their relationship continued, a cycle of pain and excuses.

What twists a man's mind to believe that violence is an answer? What sense does it make to break down the woman who holds you up? How do these relationships endure?

SEEK HELP

Before we proceed further, it is crucial to address this pressing matter. If you have recently experienced physical abuse within your relationship, I strongly urge you to seek immediate assistance from local authorities. Your safety and well-being are paramount, and prompt action can be life-saving. If contacting law enforcement feels daunting, there are dedicated Domestic Violence hotlines available to provide guidance and support tailored to your specific situation. **Please** prioritize your safety and **seek help** without hesitation.

For anyone who finds themselves becoming an abuser, **please** seek the professional help you need. If you **ever** feel you have crossed the line, take responsibility as an adult. Ignoring it will only make things worse.

MENTAL & EMOTIONAL ABUSE

₁ CONTROL FREAK

₁ There are men who have been raised believing that as men, they have full authority over every decision their woman makes. I believe a relationship should unite two <u>individuals</u> as one; I do not condone controlling behavior.

₂ Indicators of a Controlling Personality in a Relationship:

1. **Micromanagement:** Overseeing every small detail of your life and lacking trust in you to manage things independently.
2. **Perfectionism:** Setting unrealistically high standards and becoming upset when these are not met exactly.
3. **Reluctance to Delegate:** Hesitation to share responsibilities, believing they are the only one who can do things correctly.
4. **Inflexible Thinking:** Insisting that their way is the only right way, with little tolerance for your ideas or methods.
5. **Persistent Criticism:** Frequently criticizing your actions or decisions harshly to maintain control.
6. **Struggling with Uncertainty:** Becoming anxious or upset when things don't go as planned or when faced with unexpected changes.

7. **Dominating Behavior:** Controlling conversations, making decisions for you, and not allowing you to have a say.
8. **Strict Adherence to Rules:** Rigidly sticking to rules and schedules, unwilling to adapt or compromise.
9. **Compulsive Organization:** An extreme need for order and organization, often beyond what is practical or necessary.
10. **Emotional Manipulation**: Using guilt, fear, or other emotional tactics to control your behavior.

₃ These men often may try to exert control using religion, using God to enforce their rule over you or guilt you into adopting their religious beliefs, old or new. Spiritual growth as a couple is enriching; what its not is discrediting your partner because they haven't encountered the same spiritual knowledge as you have.

₄ They often fear losing control and thus feel compelled to maintain strict order, which may work well in their own lives but becomes problematic when imposed on others.

₅ This <u>fear</u> in their subconscious mind is interpreted by their conscious mind as <u>strength</u> and socially categorized as <u>manhood</u>. They believe it's a sign of a strong man, and to keep that scared little boy hidden deep in their mind, they try to make you imitate that scared little boy. Essentially, they are using you as a mirror to reflect who they truly are. How he makes you feel reflects how he feels within the depths of his mind.

6 Each drop of pain he pours onto you is a drop he *feels* he loses within himself. Unfortunately, he will never run out of drops until he addresses the true source of his pain and cuts off the faucet supplying it.

2 BREAKING HER CONFIDENCE

1 The aim here is to make you feel less than you are. Why? Because if you lack confidence in yourself, you're less likely to grow as a person, but instead grow fear that you're not good enough. These men will never give their partner enough to flourish.

2 Compliments and admiration are most meaningful when they come from someone you love and respect. When fifteen strangers tell you you're beautiful, it pales in comparison to hearing it from the one you love. What happens when society says you're *not* attractive, but the one you love and admire tells you that you're the most beautiful woman in the world?

₃ Now, consider what happens when the world tells you you're beautiful, but the one you love and admire tells you that you're no longer attractive. We tend to be more receptive and vulnerable to those we love, often without control. Yet, for the rest of the world, we can easily open and close our ears and hearts as needed.

₄ A man who uses this manipulation tactic will keep your self-confidence low, preventing you from building the courage to leave him. He might not even realize he's doing it; it could be an autopilot behavior. The mind creates habits based on what our subconscious desires, even if those habits harm others. As long as you remain in a low state, you'll never be able to leave him behind, which is exactly where he wants you to be.

₅ You must always remember that your beauty isn't based on anyone else's opinion. Including the person you love the most. Because the truth is, everyone has a base point. Meaning, their opinions are based on a building block of ideas in their brain. It's not a reality of your look; it's just a reality of how their mind has grown within society. This is why someone's opinion of you isn't totally about you. It's about their thoughts and how their brain processes what it has seen. Never take it personally, even though you're the *person* they're talking about.

₆ Your confidence will be tested. Always know that you were created with or have the ability to obtain everything you need to make it in this world. A man looking to break your confidence will try to convince you otherwise by pointing out where you're lacking.

₇ Use that as fuel. Don't view it as an insult; view it as a chisel to shape your being. If in your heart you believe his insult and you see where you can improve, do so. Improvement is a part of growing and like I always say, *"If you're not growing, you're dying."* See all criticism as fuel for growth. Because what he may not know is, he just may be creating the perfect woman to leave him.

₃ THE FINANCIAL CAGE

₁ In an old traditional household, the man brings home the bacon and the woman cooks it. Well, in many homes, that dynamic still stands. The man pays the bills, and the woman manages the house; kids included. In these household formats, they often give way to men who use their financial control as a tool of manipulation. When a person has control over your livelihood, you're often at their mercy.

₂ Many women are prevented from working, hidden under the guise of *"providing"*. These men will present themselves as traditional men who can't stand to see their woman work. These are the type of men who were raised to never let another man have dominion over his woman. He will introduce it as something beneficial to you. While this may have some truth to it, it also may become a double-edged sword in the hands of the wrong man.

3 It's a beautiful thing when a man has afforded himself the means to provide 100% of the financial burden, especially in these times! But what raises the first red flag is when you're being forced to never obtain your own means. In a healthy relationship, I believe man or woman should be allotted the freedom to pay their own taxes.

4 In a marriage particularly, I believe both adults should have access to the same accounts. Now, some women and men believe it works best for them if the more financially responsible one has sole access and that's perfectly fine. As long as both adults have the availability to retrieve enough funds in case of an emergency. Even if that emergency is running from his or her abuse.

5 Some men may have secret bank accounts or secret apartments. Any financial secrets should be questioned. While these hidden things don't automatically prove foul play, they do indicate a lack of trust between you and him. For decades, financial strain has been one of the top reasons

for divorce. The financial well-being of the family should be important to both partners.

6 For some women, their trust keeps them in the dark. They prefer to let him take control and focus on other household issues. However, I believe a team should work together in all aspects to some degree. He may lead the finances, but her having no knowledge at all is irresponsible. A man is only human; he isn't a superhero. He makes mistakes and bad decisions at times. You should have some understanding of the finances in case he is confused or unable to manage them at some point.

4 LOVE DROUGHT

1 In society, many view women as individuals who can use sexual intercourse as a tool. However, men also use love and affection as a tool to get what they want or to send a message. If you find yourself seeking love and attention from someone who usually gives it without issue, you might be experiencing a *love drought*. While there could be many reasons for his behavior, this is often the first sign.

2 When a man is upset and avoids using words because he's afraid of appearing weak and emotional, he may pull back his affection instead. This can leave you fearful of a possible

breakup, almost forcing you to bend to his desires. Once you return to the place he wants you, his affectionate self reappears.

₃ This tactic is easy for him because it requires no words and is a mental strain for the woman. He knows that if he can condition you into a state of fear, he can control your actions. Repetition conditions the brain, so the more you play his game, the better you become losing at it.

₄ The best approach is to directly address his distant behavior and lack of affection. Encourage him to use his words, assure him you hold no judgment, and remind him that you are a safe space for him to speak. Assure him you will work with him to resolve whatever he feels is wrong.

₅ Alternatively, you can fight fire with fire. When he withholds his love and affection, wait for him to come around and then become emotionally unavailable yourself.

₆ This will bring in a sense of regret for his withdrawal, *or* it can push him further out your life. Now this is the *petty* route. This is the route that has a higher probability of ending the relationship. Taking this road is for those with one foot out the door already.

₇ Don't be him, use your words.

8 His ultimate purpose of holding back his love from you is to create *"lack."* This creates desperation, and being desperate for his love is exactly what he wants.

PHYSICAL ABUSE

5 HANDS ON

1 There are many reasons men become abusive. One fact is that some of them have always had those emotions inside; they just hadn't found the outlet to express them. <u>Childhood trauma</u> is a common reason for their aggressive behavior. An abusive parent can inflict emotional scars on a child's heart. Abuse can shape a child's brain before it's fully developed, making it difficult for them to trust anyone. Imagine your first love being the source of your greatest pain. Often, therapy is needed for them to learn to express their pain with words instead of fists.

2 Having <u>conflict resolution</u> skills are essential. Many people don't know how to address their feelings properly. When you combine that with someone who, say, had a violent upbringing, it can lead to disaster in a relationship. Many women are attracted to the aggressive type—the rough-around-the-edges guy. It's natural for a woman to want a man who can protect her and her children. A perceived "Bad

Boy" appeals to her because of his protective, father-like energy.

₃ However, when this energy is held by a man whose psychological age has not progressed since childhood, it can result in a constant inner struggle; fighting to keep his emotions protected. This fight manifests itself onto you.

₄ Substance abuse often goes hand and hand with physical abuse. Alcohol and other narcotics can drive a fragile brain over the edge. These abuses can also pull out demons buried deep inside your man. This is why it's so important that every man knows not to mix those chemicals with his brain. The person it unlocks can be the person you never knew was in there.

₅ Just as with anxiety attacks from **Nessa 4:1-6** of this book, men must identify their addictions and cravings as an evil entity, something completely sperate from themselves.

₆ SHE LIKES BAD BOYS

₁ What women often mistake for protective nature is actually *emotionally unstable behavior*. Naturally, guys considered street, hood, or tough are often the most unstable. Step on their shoe in a crowded club, and they're ready to fight.

Simple words can escalate these bad boys into violence. They take big risks in the streets, and they may risk their family's safety in the same way. While eager to protect their family, knowing when not to react and taking the safest route is usually beyond them.

2 Living that lifestyle often means they're surrounded by intoxicants. Drugs in an emotionally unstable man driven by ego are a recipe for many violent moments.

3 These aggressive men often lack proper conflict resolution skills. Their go-to resolution is usually aggressive, putting themselves and their partners in avoidable situations. Their ego dictates their actions. What they call *"My Respect"* is often just their ego taking control. A man enslaved to his ego cannot truly worship God.

4 Finding a man who can calmly resolve conflicts is **valuable**. That's what you should always look for, in my opinion.

5 A man chooses the less violent option unless his or his family's lives are in danger. He uses his words to solve problems. He walks away when things get tense. He avoids actions that could keep him from seeing his family. He doesn't let his ego dictate his actions. A man doesn't risk his

life for the respect of a stranger. And a woman doesn't encourage it either.

⁷ EGO IS GOD

₁ Physical abuse isn't only perpetrated by overly aggressive men or street dudes. Some men present a calm, reserved front in public but are emotionally immature behind closed doors. Internally feeling inadequate, they feed their ego to feel alive. With God absent and their ego in control, they exert dominance over their children or partner. She loses her autonomy, and her life becomes his to control. In his eyes, he becomes her god. When he disciplines her, it's with wrath.

₂ Unable to control *himself*, he won't allow you to control *yourself* either. If you resist his control, he feels emasculated, gets emotional, and resorts to physical violence to regain control. This man is indeed less than a man, seeking control to mask his insecurities. Abusing women reveals his weakness, something he knows deep down. Controlling others lets him play god because he lacks any true godliness. Note: There are churchgoing men who also abuse women, but these type men also differ from those who *truly* live by God's teachings.

₃ For many abusers, control becomes addictive, a habit that triggers pleasure and a control high that blinds them temporarily. When the high wears off, they often apologize, confronted with their weakness. Feeling inadequate, these men may show jealousy and resentment. If they can't rise, they ensure you don't either, perhaps dragging you down to their level. The fear of losing you to a better man drives their need to dominate you. Losing their ego boost could tragically end relationships.

8 SAFE EXIT

₁ Having a safety plan is essential when in a violent relationship. Abusive individuals often cling to their emotional safety nets. Prepare *"safe words"* with trusted friends for emergencies. Identify hidden locations where you can seek refuge. Know what essential items to take if you need to escape quickly.

₂ Plan alternate routes to and from work or school and inform a trustworthy person at these locations about your situation.

₃ A useful resource for creating a safety plan is the National Domestic Violence Hotline: **thehotline.org**

₉ **POST-TRAUMATIC AWARENESS**

₁ Be mindful of the lasting effects of an abusive relationship. It can lead to anxiety and avoidance of places or things that remind you of the abuse. Depression stemming from PTSD is common and can be diagnosed.

₂ The impact of abuse can persist long after the relationship ends. If you experience sudden emotional shifts, be alert for possible triggers.

During episodes of PTSD, consider asking yourself:
- What is my current situation?
- How does my body feel?
- Who is around me? What is my environment like?
- What specific thoughts am I having?

₃ Being conscious of your surroundings and the people you are with can help identify triggers. Subconscious cues, certain situations, or environments can evoke memories of trauma, leading to unexpected sadness.

₄ Remember, their abusive behavior was a reflection of their issues, not yours. Never provoke or challenge them to harm you. Both individuals must attempt to avoid such confrontations at all costs. If possible, leave the situation and let them deal with their own misery.

Read Ashley's story again, what do you think she should do?

"A MAN ENSLAVED TO HIS EGO CANNOT TRULY WORSHIP GOD."

- MANUEL V. JOHNSON | ASHLEY 6:3

THE BOOK OF

ARIANA

DOES HE EVEN CARE

With phone in hand, Ariana hurried upstairs to her bedroom.

"Where is it?" She mumbled under her breath.

A faint voice from the phone said, *"You can just call me back when you charge it."*

>**Ariana:** "No!"
>**Bryson:** "Ok."

Bryson and Ariana had been dating for exactly 5 months, 3 weeks, and 2 days—to quote Ariana's count. For her, it had been a time of joy and completeness; she had finally gotten the man she wanted. She felt comfortable with him, allowing her vulnerable self to *be free*. She embraced every path their journey took.

Their relationship was young in nature. They dealt within their lower selves and sex was at the forefront of their connection. This immediate attraction suited Bryson perfectly, while Ariana was newer to the casual sex dating scene. Bryson navigated these waters with ease.

After months of happy moments, Ariana's feelings for Bryson deepened, and so did her expectations. She hoped his feelings would grow as hers had. However, she quickly learned that love doesn't always evolve in sync.

As her love for Bryson grew, she began to crave more from him. She wanted to plan a future together, but Bryson wasn't ready. He wasn't there for love; he wasn't there to build something lasting. And although she hadn't been either at the beginning, things changed for her.

She started discussing their future, as a test to see if he envisioned the same things she did. Bryson remained noncommittal. She planned dates and weekend getaways, but Bryson wasn't available.

Some might wonder why Ariana continued to invest in a relationship where she didn't get much in return. Bryson was the first man to genuinely make her happy, at least when they were together. But when apart, uncertainty clouded her security. The security she feels in his arms is gone when he's no longer around. When it was good, it was *great*; when it was bad, it was *terrifying.*

Ariana didn't want to seem like a nag, so she held her tongue. She didn't even know if she had the right to question him since he never labeled their relationship as heading toward something serious—they were just enjoying their time together as he put it.

Bryson was a wanted man among women in the city, and Ariana almost felt privileged that he showed interest in her. She didn't want to ruin a good thing, so she kept quiet.

It wasn't until their one-year *"situationship"* mark that things took a turn. Ariana expected some acknowledgment, perhaps a gift or special time together. But Bryson didn't even mention the day. Disappointed, she sent him a long text and he responded.

Ariana: "I'm really disappointed and saddened by the lack of care you've shown me lately. I've kept quiet about many things I've noticed, not wanting to make a fuss over trivial matters. But if I don't say anything, it will keep happening, and that's not fair to me. Today was our one-year anniversary, and I didn't hear from you. I waited all day to hear from you. If you're not into this like I am, just say so, and I'll leave you alone."

Bryson: "Anniversary is crazy."

Ariana: "You know what I meant. Is that all you got from that?"

Bryson: "I understand you're upset we didn't spend time on our 'anniversary.' I've never really celebrated things like this. Maybe if it was a one-year anniversary of a relationship or marriage, I'd pay more attention to it."

Ariana: "So what are we?"

Bryson: ... *(He paused from texting for a moment)*

Ariana: "???"

Bryson: "My bad, I stepped away from my phone."

Bryson: "I'd say we're two people who are extremely happy together and miss each other when we're apart. During that separation, we let negative thoughts cloud our minds until we reunite."

Ariana: "Do you even like me?"

Bryson: "Probably more than I should lol."

Ariana: "Whatever. When am I going to see you then?"

Bryson: "I'll come over tomorrow."

Ariana: "Ok, bae."

Bryson: "❤"

...And around...and around...they went.

₁ THE NONCHALANT GUY

₁ Have you ever dated a robot, a guy who seems to never have a care to give? While some men are naturally aloof, others are contextually aloof, depending on who they are with. This simply means that the context of their current situation can bring about this behavior. When a guy starts dating, he often gauges early on how important the connection with her is. The less important the connection, the less he shows his care. Conversely, the more important the connection, the more involved he becomes. This is why women are often right to be concerned when a man shows little effort. In the beginning I don't believe that a man should drop everything in his life to focus solely on your interests; just to be able to "read your mind" and "buy you gifts" without asking, as social media might suggest. However, I do believe a man should be attentive and gradually demonstrate through his actions that he is learning what you like and enjoy.

₂ Sadly, some men maintain long-term relationships without ever showing attentiveness to their partner. Before delving into the deeper aspects of "learning your partner," there are basic, fundamental actions that demonstrate he's paying attention to your life. Simple gestures like taking out the trash when he visits, changing a beeping smoke detector, or replacing a burnt-out light bulb show ground-level effort.

But these basic actions can be an indicator of what level man you're dealing with.

₃ Next, there are considerate actions such as putting air in your car tires, washing your car, or handling gas and oil changes. These are just a few examples of what someone who actually cares will notice and take care of. He doesn't need to know you intimately to recognize these needs; he just needs to be attuned with your well-being. His instincts should prompt him to act when he sees a full trash can. A man who's a good asset to a household that's interested in you, will make it his business to put your trash out. It's not major, but it speaks.

₄ Now all this sounds good, but the nature of your relationship has to be on par with growth. If the foundation of your connection was based around having sex, you may have signed up for a *sex-partner*, not a life partner. I wouldn't suggest looking for a man in every piece of meat. If your first conversations together were about what you'll do to each other in the bedroom, he more than likely is only going to be attentive to what you do to him *sexually*. So we have to make sure you're not looking for boyfriends in your boy toys.

₅ Often, the nonchalant attitude guys have stem from having an *abundance mindset* (See Appendix G for more details). These are men who know their worth and understand that many women would be interested in them. Whether this confidence comes from their upbringing, financial status, physique and looks, or sexual prowess, they feel assured they can easily replace you. Losing you might not be something they desire, but if it happens, they believe they can handle the consequences.

2 BIG DICK ENERGY

1 I think we're all aware of what BDE is. For those who are not, it is essentially the supreme confidence of a man who knows he can devour his female counterpart in any way she pleases. Now, BDE is supposed to be exclusive for men with large penises who have extreme faith in their sexual abilities. But as always, it has been hijacked and is now used for penis-less women and men all the same.

2 A man emitting BDE can generally come off as laid-back and unbothered. Having a calm controlled demeanor can be attractive in the eyes of most women. Seeming to never be rattled by the moment, these men allow women to rest in their feminine state. This is primarily why these men are so sought after. In today's world, women often find themselves in a masculine form to deal with society's woes. But with a man who exhibits BDE, she feels secure in her femininity.

₃ The dark side of BDE is when it becomes unhinged and drifts the line of arrogance and cockiness. When he starts to look down upon his peers as though they are no longer his human equal, that's when it becomes a nuisance. Having BDE doesn't mean you're better than anyone. It just means you recognize that no one is better than you.

₄ When his BDE leads him to become dismissive of your issues and concerns, understand that his ego may already be too far out of control. Every woman that endorses his BDE gives him another boost of confidence. He eventually develops a method of dealing with women that he's comfortable with using. Because many women have praised him while using this method, he views any woman who complains as the problem, not himself. The validation from previous women has solidified this thought process for him. So now, your concerns become *your concerns,* not his.

₅ Attempting to convince him to change his ways is almost impossible. He doesn't believe his dismissive nature is the issue because 35 women before you confirmed they had no problem with it. Half of those women loved him and accepted what they signed up for. The other half didn't care as long as they were physically pleased and had moments to bask in their femininity. You just might be the first to challenge his emotional unavailability. So, in his mind, it's 35 to 1.

3 **EMOTIONALLY UNAVAILABLE**

1 Someone whose emotions aren't available can feel like loving a brick wall. All the attention to detail you give is glossed over, and all the love you disburse is overlooked. Often, these men are categorized as selfish, but it's not always done with malicious intent.

2 A key part of being with someone is being able to share those bonding moments - those moments of intimacy that reach deeper than sex. It is imperative that we all can rest our heads on someone who can emotionally support the weight. But what happens when that support never comes?

3 Men of this fabric often avoid lengthy relationships. To be driven towards a long-term relationship, he would have to allow his *feelings* to flow through his interaction with you. If he can't *feel*, he won't **feel** the need to lock in with you long-term, even going as far as avoiding conversations aimed at a potential future with you.

4 I believe a man must be able to display empathy towards his significant other. He should be able to listen to her problems and have the ability to offer sincere consolation. Unfortunately, these types of men aren't emotionally capable. They can come off as dismissive or rude to someone who's

distressed. While that may not be their intention, it is their current character.

₅ One of the most confusing aspects of these men are the mixed signals they send. One week, they are fully committed to the relationship; the next, their communication drops off significantly. When someone lacks an emotional tie to a situation, they don't fully commit. It becomes a leisure activity for them—they indulge for their own satisfaction and then disappear again.

₆ Often, these men have multiple sexual partners. Unable to fill themselves with love, they seek fulfillment in lust. Pursuing a long-lasting relationship with such individuals can be a challenge for you.

₇ Emotionally unavailable men can also be sharp-tongued. They often speak from a place of detachment, without the emotional filter that most people use.

₈ Their inability to compromise can display traits of narcissism. Demanding control and expecting relationships to progress or end at their pace, resembles passive manipulation. A healthy relationship requires balance on both sides. These men often struggle to understand their partner's perspective, relying solely on their own viewpoint.

₉ Childhood trauma is a go-to excuse as of late. The environment our brain developed in plays a major part in how that brain functions today. Lack of a loving environment can create an unloving person.

The Loved Child

₁₀ Children who are encouraged, nurtured, and allowed to let love flow through them typically grow into love-centered adults. Their lives revolve around giving and receiving love.

₁₁ This love-centered approach influences how they function and perceive problems—through compassionate eyes. This doesn't mean they never get upset or engage in wrongdoing, but their actions are generally motivated by love. Love is their factory reset position. Their intentions are typically to bring balance and rectify situations they feel are unjust, not to cause harm or discomfort.

₁₂ Their hearts are open and vulnerable to attack. However, to fully embrace the goodness of love, one must also be open to its pain. This is why some hearts close early in life.

The Unloved Child

₁₃ Those kids who were not raised in loving environments typically turn into adults who view love as a *weakness*.

They've witnessed the pain from loving more than anything else.

14 The healthy human body is designed to avoid hurt, trauma, and death - whether voluntary or involuntary. At birth, we have a birthright through God that says we are birthed in sin through his *love*. It is only through disappointment and emotional neglect that a child develops an unhealthy relationship with love. And so, the human body does what it does best - avoids love. It offers an alternative life fuel - *survival.*

15 These kids learn to be overprotective of their emotions. Early in life, they build walls and barriers around their hearts. They manufacture defense mechanisms that allow them to survive the trauma of being separate from love.

16 The abandonment of a father, being fed lies from a mother, or worse, the death of a loved one. These are just a few of the many bricks that are cemented around a person's heart; creating no path in nor one out.

17 What this all means is, a man who is emotionally unavailable may not just be an *emotionless jerk*. He may have built a fortress around his heart due to a scarring childhood. It doesn't mean the effects of his actions don't hurt. But he has to be made aware of the source before he can change.

Low Self-Esteem

18 Low self-esteem can be an emotion killer for many. In order to fill up your woman with love, you must have some inside of you to share. If he doesn't have confidence or self-worth in himself, he can't speak it into his woman. Remember, your partner should be your support, not your drainer.

19 Feeling unprepared for the future and doubting their ability to take on the task of life are hallmarks of low self-esteem.

20 The manifestation of low self-esteem can be seen in your relationship when he doesn't show the ability to receive your love. Lack of confidence can lead to a lack of worthiness. The lack of worthiness can lead to the lack of self-love. The lack of self-love can lead to the inability to receive love. And if you have a hard time receiving love, you're probably going to have a hard time giving what you don't have… love.

21 Insecurities from a past relationship can cause an emotional block as well. It's understandable to be reserved after being hurt from a previous relationship. I'd suggest dealing with those traumas before entering a new situation. Every man and woman should want to be in a position where they can offer their best self to someone. Your best self isn't a person who's scared to love.

Previous Love

₂₂ Fear of being hurt again makes a man slow to share his love with you. Sadly, women oftentimes pay for the mistakes of women they've never met. But also, a man holding onto a past relationship can hold his emotions back from you.

₂₃ If he envisions a life with another woman, his emotional reservation with you may be due to emotionally pouring into her. Not that he is using emotion with action (physically doing things with her) to pour into her, but his heart is with her. As the saying goes, *"You can't steal second base and keep your foot on first."*

₂₄ He's going to have to come to some closure in order to love you the way you deserve. His fear of letting go of an old comfort zone can hinder his new relationship. He must understand that he's emotionally pouring into a woman who is no longer there for him to reap the benefits of all the mental and emotional currency he's giving her.

₂₅ In all of this, you're almost helpless because these are predominantly internal issues a man must tackle. But he must first be made aware of the issue. Then dig deep into himself to find the genesis of said issue.

₂₆ After you've made him aware of your concern, you can now be his support on his journey of self-discovery. Or, if he's unwilling to dive into his trauma to fix his emotional unavailability, you may consider taking a step back from the situation. We must make sure we're committed to partners that are willing to self-reflect, because that's a part of growing. As I've said throughout this book, *"If you aren't growing, you're dying."* That lack of growth can lead to an imbalance, where one partner feels inadequate and the other grows to feel like the prize.

₄ YOU'RE THE PRIZE?

₁ I've noticed there have been many debates about "The Prize". If you aren't aware, the supposed Prize is the individual in a two-person relationship who is the most valuable asset in said relationship. Men are proclaiming men as the prize and women are declaring women the same. On the surface, it may seem like just another logical assessment of a relationship. But the vainglorious way people are speaking of it, you would think they hated the very people they want to date.

₂ If you're the prize, who owns and controls you? If you're the prize, but you're **committed** to someone who isn't the prize, what does that say about you? How much value do you truly have if you've committed yourself to someone who you claim has less value than you? If you're in a serious relationship, you have value. Thus, **we all are the prize to someone** - we're all the same to someone. So, using that claim as a flex is futile.

₃ Our society finds any and every way to become combative with one another. Indulging in ego-driven conversations about how great they are. Well, that's for your wife to say; that's for your husband to say. The people you pour into will confirm your greatness or lack thereof.

₄ Many people possess great qualities, skills, and resources that others may find valuable. However, can they effectively apply these attributes to a relationship? Do they know how to share and utilize these strengths? It's like how some women speak about men with above-average physical tools betwixt their legs. You might have the tool, but can you use it effectively? The same principle applies here. You may have qualities that make you feel like you're the prize, but are you truly tested? Have you proven this theory in real situations with successful results? It's not that people can't acknowledge their value, but when it's done in a conceited manner, it diminishes the authenticity of their claim. The things you consider valuable only matter if you find someone who can appreciate and benefit from them.

5 As a society, we often place value on other people's relationships. We view breadwinners, the prettiest partner, or the most intelligent partner as the prize.

6 However, in reality, only those within the relationship can truly attest to its value. For example, I would never assume that Barack Obama is automatically the prize just because he was elected to the highest office in the world, the President of the United States. In my opinion, Michelle Obama is equally valuable to their family. In a healthy relationship, no one piece of the puzzle holds more value than the other; they all make up the bigger picture. The true mark of a healthy relationship is when both individuals recognize and proclaim the value of their partner, not just their own.

A healthy functioning relationship is the prize.

Read Ariana's story again, what do you think she should do?

"IF YOU'RE THE PRIZE, BUT YOU'RE COMMITTED TO SOMEONE WHO ISN'T THE PRIZE, WHAT DOES THAT SAY ABOUT YOU?"

- MANUEL V. JOHNSON | ARIANA 4:2

THE BOOK OF

HALLE

LEAVE THE KIDS ALONE

Halle and Maurice's eight-year rollercoaster of a relationship hit a devastating crest when they finally called it quits. Although the decision to separate was mutual, the disappointment and shame were not. Halle was a prideful woman who spoke highly of her man; some would say she placed him on a pedestal. He was always chasing a bag, in the streets regularly, which is one of the many reasons she loved him so much. He made sure she was financially secure. He was her protection from life's ills. So, you can imagine the pain she endured when she found out he was sleeping with her best friend—her heart was shattered. Halle had no idea who to turn to—her best friend betrayed her. She was ashamed to vent on social media because of the perfect image she constructed for her relationship. The world believed things were great at home because that's the way Halle wanted them to see it. But now that the cracks in her glass house began to spread, she worried it was all going to fall apart.

After weeks of begging for forgiveness and heartfelt promises of a new and improved man, Halle made the unpopular decision to forgive Maurice and stay in her relationship.

For the first six months, the new Maurice was refreshing. He was much more attentive to her concerns and far more aware of her feelings. Halle, on the other hand, was a lesser version of herself. She was clearly not the same person. She smiled through her pain, but the security she once felt before was lost. The way she allowed love to flow through her was now being filtered through mistrust and doubt. He could no longer have the best Halle because that Halle was no longer there. The primary reason they remained to-gether was Halle's fear that if she left him, her ex-best friend would have him.

The constant arguments in front of their child spread neg-ative energy throughout the home. As time drifted on, Halle and Maurice knew things were coming to an end. The energy wasn't the same. Her effort in bed wasn't there, even though he was doing more than he had ever before.

Nine months after learning of Maurice's affair, he and Halle decided to call it quits. She told people they grew apart; he told people she was crazy.

What hurt the most was when she had to tell her six-year-old son that *daddy* wouldn't be around as much anymore. She worried that staying would prevent her from being the mother her son needed to thrive. However, she also feared that leaving and raising her son without a father in the home might be equally harmful. This wasn't the first time Maurice would play a lesser role in their child's life. Run-ning the streets kept him in and out of jail, but it also kept their home furnished. The apartment they lived in was in Halle's name, so she remained, and he moved out.

He eventually moved in with her ex-best friend.

1 CHILDREN IN A BAD ENVIRONMENT

1 I feel it is our civil duty to make this planet better than it was before we got it. One of the many ways we can help with that is by giving life lessons to the children we have. Not necessarily with the gifts we give them, but with the knowledge we've learned along our journey. The love we show our kids and the love they witness will mold their minds.

2 The interactions between mother and father give a child their first representation of what communication should be like between man and woman. This is why it's important we monitor what they see and hear. From the music they listen to, to the shows they watch, to how mom and dad speak to and about one another.

3 In front of a child, your words about your relationship should be without stress and not absent of care. *"Your daddy ain't shit,"* isn't an image a child should have of their father. His father should be a kid's superhero. Most kids don't know things are bad until a parent drills it into their head. Many of us grew up poor and didn't realize it until someone told us or, more often than not, until we became adults and looked back.

₄ When you paint the picture of trash for their father figure, then tell that kid that they look like their father, they subconsciously see themselves as *trash*. They come from trash—that's their identity.

₅ *"Your mama is the reason we're in this messed-up situation."* Phrases like that from a father can build resentment in a child's psyche. The roots of future dislike for their mother can grow as they now collect data unknowingly to validate those claims.

₆ It's my opinion that parents shouldn't include children in adult trauma. Some parents love the idea of *keeping it real with my child*. I'm not a fan of this idea in the context they use it. I believe in protecting a child's innocence and preserving their childhood. Rushing kids into adulthood with the justification that they'll find out eventually is flawed logic. By that reasoning, we might as well let them have a drink of our favorite wines and liquors since, statistically speaking, they're likely to have at least one drink in their lifetime anyway. But that's obviously wrong. We separate adulthood from childhood because it's the right thing to do. Exposing children to adult problems and programming before their brains are fully developed can have adverse effects.

7 Sharing your stresses with a child is dumping negative energy into a child. Your child is not your therapist. Albert Einstein said, *"Energy cannot be created or destroyed, it can only be changed from one form to another."* With us knowing this, what do you think happens to the sadness and negative thoughts you pour into your child? Notice if you feel better after you vent to your kid about his father/mother. You've released your dragging energy onto your child. It's not always only about you *getting something off your chest.* It's about what you're putting on theirs.

8 You may feel you're just preparing them for the hardships of life, but you may just be initiating them *into* the hardships of life. I've seen parents particularly in my ethnic group purposely mold their kids into *tough little guys* who hate law and order. They claim they're preparing them for the rough world of the streets. While that sounds noble, I'd counter that by suggesting you prepare them to avoid the streets first and foremost. Teaching a kid to survive in the streets is one thing but teaching them to avoid the streets altogether is another.

9 I understand that things happen, and adults fall on hard times. But that has less to do with learning to be *street smart* and more to do with learning to be *financially smart*. You dress for the job you want, not for the job you have. It's good to teach your child what to do when the lights cut off. It's

great to teach your child how to make sure the lights never cut off. Many parents miss the latter.

2 BOUNDARIES BETWEEN PARENTS

1 Co-parenting has become such a normal occurrence it almost seems to be the first option the minute the child is born. While no one truly goes into parenthood wanting to be a single parent, life happens, relationships end, and one becomes two again.

2 While we practice protecting our children's innocence, we must try to balance the daily disappointment we're experiencing from our failed relationship. When love is severed between two individuals, there's a period of uncertainty. We can't pass this uncertainty on to our children. Boundaries and guidelines must be established between the two individuals.

3 Breaking up for a legitimate reason and then ignoring that reason by continuing to have sex only worsens the problem. If the issue can be fixed, let's fix it. But if it can't, we need to move on. We can't break up and try to preserve only the good feelings. Holding on by a thread will cause a devastating fall when it snaps. If you're letting go, let it go.

₄ The reason you sometimes try to maintain a sexual connection is that it provides a sense of harmony during an inharmonious time. You're seeking the *good* in a *bad* situation rather than addressing the bad roots that sprouted this turmoil. This might be because deep down you both understand that the problems can't be easily resolved. And so, you both ignore them, bypassing the difficult task in front of you.

₅ Expectations as parents need to be discussed. Things such as:

- The time your child spends in each household.
- The foods your child is allowed to eat.
- Advanced/timely notifications of visitation or pick-up.
- Finances/who pays what.

Just the basics, but these will vary based on your individual circumstances. However, it is essential that they are addressed and established for proper co-parenting.

₆ If you're dealing with a man who resists setting guidelines and boundaries, it can make things challenging. Perhaps you and he are not on the same journey, resulting in different outlooks. If both of you are positive influences for the child, your goals should align, even if your approaches differ. You can't force the father to think like you, but you can ensure that you instill the values and qualities you want your child to uphold.

7 For example, you may be against a heavy sugar-based diet, while their father may not care. Explain to your child the downsides of consuming too much sugary food, show them educational videos on the topic, and have their teacher reinforce this message. This way, when the father offers them candy, they won't be as eager to eat the entire box in one sitting.

8 In most cases, all you can do is your part. A bad parent, along with the influences of the physical and digital worlds, may try to lead your child astray. Your job is to ensure you don't join them in that negative influence.

3 INCOMING INCARCERATION

1 Sometimes the person you choose to have children with doesn't choose to make the right decisions. Or sometimes you know exactly the type of man you signed up for. Either way, the decisions we make as parents not only affect us, but also those closest to us. So when a man does anything that can risk his freedom and push him to be an absentee parent, we have to question his reasoning.

₂ Crime is undeniably bad, but not all crimes are equal. If they were, everyone would receive the same sentence for every offense. When considering why a father is absent from his child's life, we need to understand the reasons behind his actions. A parent's judgment is crucial to a child's development. If a parent can't keep themselves safe, how can they ensure their child's safety?

₃ Children should be raised in secure homes. Your home should be a sanctuary for your child, shielding them from the world's troubles. If a mother or father fails to provide a safe environment, they must make necessary adjustments to their living conditions.

₄ When a father is incarcerated and the child is left without one parent, the mother must assume both roles—nurturer and disciplinarian. Depending on the length of the father's absence, she may become the child's primary mentor and guide.

₅ It is a significant challenge for a woman to manage everything alone. I recommend that any mother raising a son ensures he has positive male influences in his life. Brothers, cousins, and other male relatives of yours can step in as father figures, providing the child with a sense of what manhood entails. It is essential for every young boy to have positive older male influences around him.

₆ I don't believe the guy you met last week at the club, even if he has a good job, should be involved in your child's life. Such relationships are uncertain, and uncertainty is not beneficial for any child. Your child doesn't need to meet your new fling every month. We don't want them forming bonds with men who might vanish from their life. Instead, family members who share his bloodline typically have a deeper sense of care and responsibility.

₇ Dealing with a man who is incarcerated can be challenging. Beyond the difficulties of parenthood, feelings of loneliness and abandonment may trigger past traumas if you've experienced similar losses before. Some women stay the course, some move on immediately, and others break down over time. Every situation is unique. However, if you chose this lifestyle, you must be prepared for when things go downhill. It's unfair to support a man when he's doing wrong and then abandon him when consequences arise. Commitment goes beyond faithfulness; it means being dedicated to a cause or activity. Therefore, committing to someone also means embracing the lifestyle they lead. These situations are not one-size-fits-all, and many factors do play a role.

₈ If you knew this was part of the deal, treat it accordingly. If you weren't aware of his criminal activities and this comes as a shock, it's understandable to take a different approach. You never committed to that lifestyle, and you shouldn't be expected to endure it. Choosing to stay would be commendable at that point.

₉ Ultimately, the most important factor in any decision is what's best for you and your child. Any man behind bars should understand and agree with that.

₄ PRISON PROMISES

₁ Beware of the *Prison Promises*. The fast life can be a wild race, and when it comes to a sudden stop, it can jolt a man's mind. This pause often gives men an opportunity for clarity and self-reflection, allowing them to dwell on regrets and missteps, the people they've wronged, and the advice they've ignored.

₂ During these dark hours, many men reach out to those who will keep them afloat. Given that a woman's natural state is to nurture, they often become the prime targets. There's nothing inherently wrong with seeking support in times of need; we all *need* help at some point. The problem arises when he creates a facade of love out of thin air. He hasn't had a genuine change of heart or a moment of true reflection. Instead, he uses her strong attachment to him to his advantage. Fortunately for him, this manipulation isn't a crime.

₃ Many men with girlfriends make a concerted effort to keep these women in their lives while incarcerated. They understand that *"out of sight, out of mind"* can be a dagger to their relationship. Their goal is to constantly reassure her that things will improve and/or return to normal soon. If *normal* wasn't good, the objective shifts to convincing her that things will be *better* once he is released.

₄ Have you ever heard these oh-so-famous lines?

- *"We're gonna get married when I come home."*
- *"When I get home, things will be different."*
- *"I've been reading every day."*
- *"I'm going to keep a job this time."*
- *"I found God."*
- *"I learned my lesson."*
- *"I want to be there for my son/daughter."*
- *"I think we can make things work this time."*
- *"It's all about my family when I get home."*

I can go on for pages. But if you've been in this situation, I'm sure you've heard one of these. Even the guilt trip phase:

- *"You can see other men if you want."*

This is only said to prompt you to respond with, *"No! I only want you."* It's a classic example of <u>reverse psychology</u>.

₅ While all these lines may be true in theory, they often fall short in reality. Prison walls have a way of driving a man insane. So much so, he will forget that his words and intentions have to be tested against the temptations of the outside world. So it's not an open-and-shut case like he may think.

₆ I wouldn't say you should dismiss all his promises as deception. Many men do learn from their mistakes. Just make sure he puts his right hand on the Bible when he says it.

₅ DEATH OF A PARENT

₁ Life throws curveballs at us all the time. Circumstances arise that are seemingly out of our control. It's hard being a single parent; it's even harder being the surviving parent of a now half-orphan.

₂ I had one young lady tell me that she'd rather her son's father be dead. At least she'd know it wasn't a choice to be an absentee parent. I reminded her that it doesn't matter how *she* feels. How would the child feel? I had to explain to her that childhood scars may last a long time if not checked.

But death is forever, and there's no fixing it. There is no re-demption for the father. There is no reclamation of their relationship.

3 Understand your child and their father can always make amends later in life, and it could be beneficial. Personally, my father and I didn't have our strongest bond until I reached 35 years old, and I'm thankful it happened. So just because you and the father will never be together doesn't mean he and his child will never be together.

4 We need to be cautious about how we inform our kids of a tragedy. Some parents are very direct, while others avoid the conversation entirely. I believe that when our kids start asking questions, we should follow God's example and give them only as much information as their young minds can handle, in a way that they can understand.

5 In my opinion, we should portray a lost parent as a symbol of strength for our child. I believe it can be more harmful than helpful to "tell all" and be "100% real" with them. Personally, I don't mind telling kids the tooth fairy is real. Allowing children to remain in their innocent, childlike mindset is something that society is missing. Social media has already stripped them of that gift; don't contribute to it. Again, I believe shielding children from traumatizing events is better for their development.

———

₆ When it's all said and done, as the great comedian Chris Rock once said, *"You can drive a car with your feet if you want to, that don't make it a good fucking idea."* You can raise your child alone; it doesn't always mean that's best for the child. But when the other parent causes more harm than help to the child's development, alone might be better.

₇ When tragedy strikes and a child loses their father, it's even more important to shield them from our stress and let them remain children. Despite the absence of a father, the child's hero can still live on.

Read Halle's story again, what do you think she should do?

"YOU'RE SEEKING THE *GOOD* IN A *BAD* SITUATION RATHER THAN ADDRESSING THE BAD ROOTS THAT SPROUTED THIS TURMOIL."

- MANUEL V. JOHNSON | HALLE 2:4

THE BOOK OF

OH! THE DISRESPECT

L ife grew increasingly challenging for Ava as Aiden's behavior took a bizarre turn. The emotional connection they once shared seemed to evaporate, leaving Ava feeling lost and disconnected. She couldn't shake the feeling that something was off, noticing the subtle shifts in Aiden's demeanor, his distant gaze, and lack of physical affection. The man who once adored her seemed like a stranger; his warm touch replaced by cold indifference. Ava was suffocating. Her best friend, Charity, seemed to be her rock during these troubling times. Charity frequently urged Ava to leave Aiden, insisting that he wasn't good for her. *"You deserve so much better,"* Charity would say, her eyes filled with concern. Despite Charity's constant warnings, Ava found it hard to let go of him, hoping things would return to the way they once were.

The turning point came on a rainy night when Ava's intuition screamed for answers she could no longer ignore. With trembling hands, she decided to investigate Aiden's phone. Her heart raced as she unlocked it, hoping to find nothing but fearing the worst. What she discovered shattered her world—Aiden had been engaging in malicious gossip, spreading lies about her to their social circle through text. Suddenly, friends whom she once trusted began to treat her differently, their doubtful glances amplifying her sense of isolation. Whispers followed her everywhere; each one a reminder of the lies Aiden had spun.

Adding insult to injury, Aiden's friends, sensing her vulnerability, attempted to insert themselves into Ava's life, further undermining her sense of security and trust. Their sly remarks and flirtatious advances only deepened Ava's wounds. It felt as if the walls were closing in, every familiar face now a potential threat.

Confronting Aiden about his actions brought little closure. Despite his apologies, which seemed hollow in the face of his deceit, Ava found herself standing alone, wounded by the betrayal of the one person she believed she could rely on.

Aiden's claims of wanting to be with her rang false, his actions consistently betraying his words. He made no genuine effort to win her back, his empty promises serving only to salt her wounds.

As Ava struggled to rebuild her shattered life, she found an unexpected ally in her best friend, Charity. Charity had been telling Ava for months to leave Aiden, insisting he wasn't good for her. Charity's constant warnings echoed in Ava's mind as she tried to make sense of the betrayal.
But one day, Ava stumbled upon a series of new texts on Charity's phone that revealed a sinister truth. Charity had

not been looking out for Ava's best interests. Instead, she had been plotting to take Aiden for herself. Her seemingly protective advice was a manipulative tactic to drive a wedge between Ava and Aiden, ensuring that Aiden would eventually fall into her waiting arms.

The realization hit Ava like a freight train. Charity, the person she had confided in, the one she thought was her staunchest ally, had been betraying her all along. It wasn't just Aiden's betrayal that cut deep; it was Charity's deception that truly broke her. The friend she had trusted with her deepest fears and insecurities had been scheming behind her back, driven by selfish desires.

With a newfound strength, Ava confronted Charity. The confrontation was explosive, emotions running high as the truth spilled out. Charity, caught off guard, tried to justify her actions, but there was no justification that could mend the deep wounds she had inflicted.

In that moment, Ava realized she was better off without both Aiden and Charity. She walked away from the toxic entanglements that had suffocated her for so long. As she stepped into the night, she felt a weight lift off her shoulders. The scars would remain, but she was no longer defined by them. Ava was free, and for the first time in a long time, she could breathe.

₁ HE DOESN'T FIND ME SEXY ANYMORE

₁ It's natural to seek validation and desire from our partners, especially in terms of feeling sexy and attractive. However, there may come a time when you notice a shift in your man's perception of your attractiveness. While this can be disheartening, it's essential to understand that attraction dynamics are complex and multifaceted.

₂ Communication Breakdowns

A common reason your partner might not find you as sexy as before could be due to communication issues. Over time, couples might become lax in expressing their needs and desires. This can lead to misunderstandings and a slow erosion of attraction.

₃ Initially, couples often communicate openly about their desires and preferences. But as time goes on, these conversations may become less frequent. This lack of communication can create a gap, leaving important needs unmet and intimacy diminished.

₄ When unspoken expectations build up, they can weaken the connection between partners. If your partner feels unheard or misunderstood, it can affect their engagement in intimate moments, leading to a decline in attraction. This process is gradual and often unnoticed until the emotional distance becomes significant.

₅ To address this, prioritize open and honest communication. Create opportunities to discuss your desires and fantasies in a supportive environment. Encourage your partner to share their thoughts and listen actively. You and he should be not only lovers but also close friends. Effective communication doesn't need to be as complicated as you both might be making it.

₆ **Familiarity and Comfort**
Another factor is the idea that familiarity can breed comfort. In long-term relationships, partners become very familiar with each other's habits and appearance, which can sometimes lead to a decrease in the thrill of discovery and desire. Hearing your significant other use the toilet can leave a sound in your mind that's harder to flush than the toilet itself.

₇ As you share experiences and support each other through life's challenges, your bond strengthens, providing a stable foundation for love. However, this emotional closeness can sometimes make physical attraction feel less exciting. The spontaneous adventures that characterized the early days of your relationship might be replaced by routines.

₈ While stability and security are valuable, they can also dampen the flames of passion. <u>Predictable</u> activities and interactions can reduce the element of surprise that *fuels* attraction. Your once vibrant connection might start to feel <u>stagnant</u>, leading to dissatisfaction and a longing for something new.

₉ To keep the passion alive, introduce spontaneity into your relationship. Surprise your partner with unexpected acts of affection, like love notes or impromptu dates. Or simply give him a relaxing massage after a long day. Use scented oils or lotions to make it more special. Embrace new activities and adventures together to keep things exciting and fresh.

₁₀ **External Stressors**

Work pressures, financial concerns, or family obligations, can also impact a person's libido and interest in intimacy. When overwhelmed by external stresses, your man might unknowingly neglect your need for affection and validation, leading to feelings of unattractiveness.

₁₁ High-stress jobs, financial instability, and other worries can consume mental energy, leaving little room for intimacy. The stress can also manifest in irritability or criticism.

₁₂ **Evolving Together**

Life's stresses can lead you to adopt new habits and ways of thinking to cope and grow. As a woman, you evolve, learn more about yourself, and experience life in various changing ways. While these changes may seem harmless, the man who once gave you physical attention may also notice these changes and may not always approve of the new you.

₁₃ This isn't to suggest that you should live your life by his rules. However, it is important to remember that a relationship isn't a solo endeavor. Your partner is your other half, and you guys decisions should reflect that shared journey.

₁₄ Being your own woman and moving at your own pace is empowering, but it's also crucial to understand that independent decision-making comes with consequences.

₁₅ If you have changed from the woman your man originally fell in love with, it may take him some time to look beyond the surface and rediscover the heart and soul of the woman he once adored so dearly.

₁₆ Ultimately, your worth is not defined by external validation but by the love and respect you have for yourself. Life can cloud perceptions, but the heart's true feelings persist. Remember, any changes in his attraction towards you may *not necessarily* be due to you changing; it could be due to a shift in his perception. But if you do in fact see a different woman when you look in the mirror, so does he.

₂ HE HAD SEX WITH MY BEST FRIEND

₁ Nothing can twist the knife in your back more than someone you trusted who's sleeping around on you. Except for when it's with another person you also trusted.

₂ This feeling of betrayal is unlike any other, striking at the very core of your being. What would drive a man to stoop so low and share himself in this way?

₃ Often when a man cheats in general, it's not always because he lacks love and respect for you, though that can and often is the case. More often, he lacks love and respect for the bond you two share. It's the relationship he disregards. This is why, during arguments, he might plead his case, insisting he still loves you. Subconsciously, he feels he violated the terms of the relationship, not you as a person. While this may sound absurd, it provides insight into how a man's mind can sometimes process these situations.

₄ When a man *lacks discipline*, he falls to every temptation, indulging in every fleeting pleasure to satisfy his cravings. He loses himself in his lust, which spirals beyond his control. At times this lack of restraint leads him to make decisions he consciously knows he shouldn't, yet he does them anyway. He becomes a slave to temptation and, ultimately, to the darker forces that govern those urges.

₅ Once he becomes a slave to his urges, there is no limit to what he might do. The extent of his infidelity reflects the depth of his enslavement. A man who succumbs to the temptation of sleeping with someone close to you may not be *entirely* under the spell of his desires, but he is dangerously close.

₆ From his perspective, sleeping with someone close to you might have seemed effortless, particularly if your friend was equally willing. Consider whether you've ever shared intimate details about his prowess in bed with your friend or mentioned your friend's promiscuous behavior to him. Telling your homegirl how big he is and telling your man how freaky your friend can get, oftentimes heightens intrigue. These conversations could have influenced his actions.

₇ I always advise women **never** to tell their partner about other women who find him attractive or who are sexually adventurous. Doing so only piques his curiosity. While it's true that a committed man shouldn't stray regardless of what you tell him, life isn't always that straightforward. We must ensure we're upholding our side of the relationship be-cause that's the only part we can control.

₈ Conversely, I always advise women **never** to tell their close friends and relatives how good their man is in bed. You don't want to spark their curiosity. Keep what happens behind your bedroom door private and ensure that what occurs outside those doors stays outside.

₃ HE SAYS HE STILL WANTS ME... HE'S LYING

₁ No one truly wants to be the cause of a breakup, even if they initially desired the separation. It's natural for some men to try to mend what they've broken, not because they've changed or learned their lesson, but because they can't live with being the reason it ended.

₂ These men will plead for the relationship to continue, insisting that things will be different. In reality, they're often just trying to end the current moment on a better note. This is why immediate apologies can feel insincere. A genuine apology requires self-reflection and a commitment to change. It involves building the discipline to avoid the behaviors that led to the situation. An immediate apology, if not sincere, is often just a way to stop your tears because he believes that's what you need to hear.

₃ They would prefer the breakup to seem mutual so they can tell their new partner, *"We just grew apart,"* rather than admitting, *"I cheated, and she left me."* Which one sounds less like a red flag to you?

₄ Another reason he may say he wants you when he doesn't might be attributed to the thoughts of seeing you with someone else, often stemming from a fear of being exposed as inadequate. The fear that you'll find a man with the discipline needed for a healthy relationship highlights his own weaknesses and lack of self-control.

₅ It's often said that men don't want someone else having sex with their former partner. This might hold true for men who *knew* they weren't satisfying their woman in bed, but more often, it's the fear of someone else providing emotional support, stability, and respect that scares them the most.

₆ Whether his reasons for pleading to get back together are due to not wanting to end things on a bad note or fear of his shortcomings being exposed, if he hasn't conquered his urges, nothing significant will change. Without developing new levels of self-discipline, any reconciliation is likely to be temporary. He's ultimately the same man.

₇ Learning his lesson isn't about feeling remorseful for cheating; it's about mastering his impulses and eliminating the issues that led to the betrayal. This is why tears mean nothing. Women often believe that learning his lesson means he felt the pain she experienced. He may understand the immediate pain, but once she takes him back, the lesson stops. The real lesson is in developing strategies to control those urges and implementing them consistently.

₈ If he can't tell you or demonstrate the methods he's practicing to manage his desires, you shouldn't even consider taking him back.

₄ HIS FRIENDS ARE NOW HITTING ON ME

₁ After a breakup, it's not uncommon for your ex's friends to express interest in dating you. There are several reasons why this might happen, but one thing is clear: they disregard the unwritten rule against dating a friend's ex and lack respect for your boundaries.

₂ If your ex spoke highly of you to his friends, this could explain their sudden interest. While sharing intimate details with friends and family is generally ill-advised, if your ex did so, his friends might have listened attentively, fueling their curiosity and eagerness to pursue you.

₃ Another factor could be ego. If they admire your ex, being with someone he once had could make them feel like they're on his level. This behavior is common among both men and women, similar to individuals who boast about sleeping with celebrities to elevate their status. It's a way of seeking validation and recognition from their peers, much like how a good credit score can make lenders more willing to offer favorable terms. If they feel sleeping with you raise their social stock, they will take on the opportunity.

₄ Moreover, his friends might have seen how he treated you behind the scenes and concluded that he didn't truly care about you. If your ex disrespected you behind your back, his friends might feel justified in pursuing you now, seeing an opportunity where respect and boundaries have already been eroded by your ex.

₅ Lastly, it is possible they harbored an attraction towards you all along but respected the invisible boundaries imposed by your relationship. Now that these barriers have dissolved, they see an opening to act on their long-held feelings.

₆ While there can be various reasons why your ex's friends may hit on you after a breakup, these actions often reflect a lack of respect for boundaries and social norms. It's essential to recognize their motives and prioritize your own comfort and well-being.

₅ THE GOSSIP KING

₁ It's a deeply unbecoming trait for a man to expose his woman's shortcomings, be it men or women. Even worse is the act of spreading falsehoods and blatant lies to garner sympathy within social circles.

₂ This often occurs when men fail to treat their woman as their closest confidant. This dynamic leaves the woman feeling detached, separate from him despite their togetherness. In such a disconnected relationship, her problems remain hers alone, and his problems remain his own, further widening the emotional gap.

₃ When a relationship is bound by a proper, deep connection, how one's significant other is perceived by others is very important. A man should prioritize his own view of his woman, but also care about how she is perceived among her peers. His feelings for her matters first, but he should make sure the world knows how wonderful she is as well. If nobody can tell her story in a positive light, he can. This protective instinct stems from love and respect. While we often tell ourselves that self-perception is all that matters, we cannot ignore that we share this planet with eight billion others. Our social standing and the respect we command are ultimately shaped and judged by the perceptions of those around us.

4 The true essence of a relationship lies in the fragile balance between self-perception and societal perception. We navigate a world where our interactions and reputations are shaped by both *intimate bonds* and *public opinions*. Understanding this delicate interplay is key to forming relationships that not only withstand personal trials but also thrive in the broader social landscape. So, in a world where *perceptions* can shape destinies, it is our <u>sacred duty</u> to cherish and safeguard the honor of those we love. For in doing so, we not only elevate their standing in the eyes of others but also affirm our own integrity and the authenticity of our shared journey.

5 Protecting your woman's reputation is literally apart of being her man. It's not just about physical protection.

6 So when a man talks bad about his woman, it says more about *him* than it does *her*. This distinction is crucial for anyone in a relationship, as it helps to see mistreatment for

what it truly is: a manifestation of the perpetrator's inner turmoil and not a reflection of the victim's value. This perspective empowers individuals to recognize their own worth and realize the worthlessness of the person talking about them.

Read Ava's story again, what do you think she should do?

"...WHEN A MAN TALKS BAD ABOUT HIS WOMAN, IT SAYS MORE ABOUT *HIM THAN* IT DOES *HER*."

- MANUEL V. JOHNSON | AVA 5:6

THE BOOK OF

LESLIE

HOW GOOD IN BED IS HE REALLY

L eslie, at 32, found herself increasingly disheart- ened by her sex life with Jon. Each sexual en- counter had become a dull routine, stripping away any traces of passion. She longed for a connection that went beyond the ordinary, yet Jon's mechanical and uncaring approach only deepened her sense of isolation. His routine questions about her satisfaction felt more like checkpoints than expressions of genuine care. The words, *"Did you cum?"* linger painfully in her memories.

The lack of enthusiasm during oral sex further compounded Leslie's frustration. It wasn't just about the physical act; it was the yearning for a bond that reached beyond the surface. The bedroom, once a haven of closeness, had turned into a piercing reminder of unmet needs and unspoken disappointments.

Leslie's emotions became a tangled web of confusion and self-doubt. She questioned whether her dissatisfaction stemmed from poor choices in partners or something inherently wrong within herself. This internal conflict gnawed at her, leading to guilt-ridden thoughts of ending the relationship solely due to bad sex.

In her quiet moments, Leslie began a journey of self-reflection. She sought to understand if she truly deserved a love that was both passionate and understanding. The routine of their encounters served as a mirror, reflecting the harsh reality of her choices. She stood at a crossroads, faced with the painful decision of settling for less or daring to pursue the kind of intimacy she deeply craved. As her inward searching deepened, she came to a sobering realization:

perhaps, her experiences were shaped not just by the men she chose, but by her own evolving understanding of what she truly needed. She was learning herself and within that, she realized the things that stimulated her before were maybe no more.

₁ THE *CAN AND WANT* THEORY

₁ Many single women struggle with not feeling a deep physical connection despite being involved with a man. This issue can be better understood through the "Can and Want Theory," which explores the dynamics of sexual satisfaction and partner selection.

₂ The theory states that men may not fully sexually satisfy women because they are often settling for the easy sexual options available to them rather than pursuing those they truly desire. Men often give less effort in bed when it's with a woman they got in bed with ease. Typically, because the woman that came with ease is the woman that wanted him more than he wanted her. This difference in his sexual approach leads to varying levels of effort and engagement in bed.

₃ Society suggests that women tend to be more selective in choosing sexual partners. They often engage with men they genuinely desire, which makes their encounters more meaningful and attentive. These women are not necessarily more satisfied, but they tend to put in more effort because they care about the man they're intimate with. Meaning, this is the man they truly wanted to sleep with, not just the available option.

4 Men don't always choose partners based on desire. Instead, at times they may settle for the women who are available, leading to <u>less effort</u> and attentiveness in these sexual encounters. This behavior from men stems from their comfort with women at or *below* their social status, while women typically aim for partners at or *above* their social status. Men are more prone to sleep with someone they have no attraction to, outside of them having a vagina.

5 This dynamic produces a lack of effort from men who don't feel the need to impress women they are not genuinely interested in. As a result, these women experience less-than-satisfactory physical and emotional intimacy because their partners are not fully invested.

6 Societal norms also play a role. Women are often socialized to seek meaningful connections and long-term relationships, whereas men might prioritize availability and convenience in their sexual encounters. This mismatch can lead to a disconnect in the bedroom, with women feeling

unfulfilled and men not realizing the depth of effort required to satisfy their partners.

7 In short, if he's not putting forth the effort to please you in bed, it might be because he doesn't see you as being his equal. If he's only sleeping with you because you're always available or you were available at the time, not because you were his ultimate choice, his lack of commitment and effort will show. When people settle, they often don't take the relationship as seriously, nor do they put in the necessary work to make it fulfilling. We must recognize our own needs and not settle for less than what we truly desire.

8 The *Can and Want Theory* highlights the importance of genuine desire and effort in sexual satisfaction. By being more selective and communicating needs clearly, women can create deeper connections and more fulfilling intimate experiences. But keep in mind, if he feels you're replaceable, he may replace you. That's okay though. He's just giving you room for the man who truly desires you.

₂ LISTEN TO HER BODY

₁ Too often, men draw misguided conclusions from porn, assuming that what they saw on film is an indication of how they should approach sex with their partner. Clearly oblivious to the fact that much of it is performed for theatrical effect—a commercialized experience. Some believe that forceful and aggressive thrusts equate to satisfying sex, while others think rapid strokes lead to climax. While these approaches may give results at times, they should not be the **sole standard** for pleasing *every* woman.

₂ A man should take on the fluidity of water, allowing himself to be guided by a woman's body. Bedtime should be like navigating a winding river, smoothly adapting to each turn in unison. Failure to do so may result in *crashing* against the riverbank's edge. While the destination may be reached, the journey's enjoyment is compromised.

₃ Many men attempt to impose their preferred sexual style universally. While it may resonate with some, it may not for others. A willingness to embrace diverse forms of physical stimulation is crucial for satisfying a sexual partner. Exploring new avenues of pleasure is not just about personal experience; it's about ensuring mutual enjoyment in a successful intimate session. A man must be willing to adjust to a woman's need. *Listen to her body.*

₄ Why does this take place? More often than not, these men have separated intimacy from sex. While intimacy can stand alone without sex, sex without intimacy is less personal for a woman. But for a man who has completely separated the two, the final destination of ejaculation is the goal, and intimacy isn't necessary.

₅ Many times, a man may disregard a woman's orgasm if he lacks genuine care for her. If his concern is solely self-directed, his actions in bed will reflect that self-centeredness. The desire to provide a great sexual experience requires selflessness, a quality absent in someone who doesn't care.

₆ Additionally, if he senses that you are only having sex with him because he desires to, he might prioritize his own satisfaction during the encounter. Therefore, it's important to be mindful of your response to his attempts to sleep with you. Responding with an indifferent attitude like, *"Okay, fine, but keep it down this time,"* could lead him to perceive the sexual encounter as a mere task, similar to how one might treat an exchange with a prostitute. This leads him to believe that you've already dismissed the idea of enjoying the moment, so he won't push the issue by attempting to *make* you enjoy it. If you act like you don't want it, he will act like you don't deserve it.

3 **EMOTIONAL INTIMACY**

1 In a relationship, one aspect often holds the key to a truly fulfilling connection: emotional intimacy. This foundational element forms the bedrock upon which trust, understanding, and lasting bonds are built.

2 At its core, emotional intimacy involves the mutual sharing of thoughts, feelings, and vulnerabilities between partners. It goes deeper than the surface level of companionship, reaching into the profound understanding that binds two individuals. This connection lays the groundwork for a relationship that enriches both partners in ways that extend far beyond the surface.

3 A crucial aspect of creating emotional intimacy is effective communication. The ability to express thoughts

and feelings openly, without fear of judgment, is important. This communication delves into the inner workings of emotions, aspirations, and fears that shape our individual experiences.

₄ To build emotional intimacy, it is essential to **actively listen** to one another. Listening involves more than hearing words; it requires an attentive awareness of emotions, nuances, and unspoken cues. When partners **feel** heard and understood, a profound sense of connection flourishes, paving the way for emotional intimacy to live.

₅ Vulnerability is another key element in nurturing emotional closeness. Opening up to another person, exposing fears and insecurities, requires trust. This trust forms a bridge connecting individuals on a deeper emotional level, building an environment where both partners feel secure enough to be themselves–an environment void of judgment.

₆ In the pursuit of emotional intimacy, creating shared experiences is vital. Whether significant milestones or simple day-to-day interactions, these moments contribute to the fabric of connection. They create lasting memories that bind individuals together, strengthening emotional bonds.

7 Empathy plays a pivotal role in building emotional intimacy. It involves understanding and sharing each other's feelings, creating a connection based on mutual compassion. Engaging in empathetic exchanges bridges the gap between individual experiences, deepening understanding of each other's emotional landscapes.

8 Nurturing emotional intimacy is an ongoing process that requires dedication from both partners. It is dynamic, evolving with the relationship. Regular check-ins, open conversations about emotions, and a commitment to mutual growth contribute to its sustained development over time.

9 Building richer emotional connections with each other will create richer moments in bed. When two people are emotionally strangers, this often manifests as a lack of intimacy for many women during intercourse. The more you understand a person's life, the more you care. The more you care, the deeper the bond. And the deeper the bond, the better the bedroom.

₄ **UNMET PHYSICAL DESIRES**

₁ Sometimes, guys end up focusing more on their own pleasure during sex, leaving women feeling unsatisfied. There are a few reasons why this happens.

₂ If there isn't enough talk about preferences, assumptions can lead to a one-sided experience. Guys can't read minds, so openly discussing likes, boundaries, and fantasies is crucial. Don't be afraid to tell him what you like. You don't have to be direct if that's not your way of handling things. Honestly, being indirect often goes over better.

₃ Which sentence do you feel a man will embrace more?

1. "Ooou bae, I want you to go slow inside of me tonight!"
2. "I don't like the way you go so fast inside of me!"

Sentence 1 is likely to get a better and more proactive reaction from most men. In contrast, Sentence 2 is likely to put him on the defensive, feeling as though his manhood is under attack.

₄ Societal expectations about masculinity often pressure men to focus on performance rather than mutual satisfaction. This can create a disconnect, where the emphasis is on how well they perform by societal standards instead of how well he makes his *actual* woman **feel.**

₅ A lack of knowledge is another common issue. Some men might not fully understand female anatomy or what brings pleasure. Comprehensive sex education for everyone can dispel myths and ensure mutual satisfaction. It's hard to climb a mountain when you don't know the path. Watching videos on the topic together can allow you to say less and permit the video to speak for you.

₆ Insecurities play a significant role in sexual relationships. When a man has performance issues, he may focus solely on maintaining his erection. As he concentrates on getting through the session before his erection falters, he misses the opportunity to please his partner. This focus on his own anxiety and performance prevents him from being fully present and attentive to his partner's needs and desires, ultimately affecting the intimacy and satisfaction of the experience for her. To get over this, he needs assurance that it's okay and less ridicule for his insufficiencies.

₇ In summary, one-sided focus on a man's pleasure in bed often stems from communication issues, social expectations, lack of education, and insecurity. Open communication, breaking societal pressures, and improved sex education can help you build a more balanced and satisfying sexual experience together. Addressing these issues with femininity can piece things together gracefully.

₅ DOWNTOWN

₁ Oral sex is often hailed as one of humanity's greatest discoveries. Okay, that might be an exaggeration, but it's widely acknowledged that when performed skillfully, it can transform into an extraordinary experience. Many women go through life without fully experiencing the satisfaction of oral pleasure, causing some to gradually lose interest in this intimate act.

₂ Understanding the dynamics of sexual exploration, especially when it comes to oral sex, can be complex. There could be several reasons why he isn't pleasing you orally.

HERE ARE A FEW TO CONSIDER:

3 The Look for Licks

Among men, close conversations often revolve around their sexual experiences. For many men, a crucial factor in whether they perform oral sex on you may hinge on your appearance. Your level of physical attractiveness can influence the sexual pleasure you receive. It's important to recognize that you may be appealing enough for sex but not necessarily for oral. Women often base their sexual advances on emotional intimacy or how they're treated. Meanwhile, some men gauge their interest based on physical allure. This perspective is *more* common among younger men but remains a perspective nonetheless for men of any age group.

4 Keeping It Clean

Hygiene is crucial. Some men might hesitate due to concerns about cleanliness. Good personal hygiene is appreciated by everyone and enhances intimate moments. Both partners should prioritize cleanliness, which creates a refreshing sexual experience. Openly discussing preferences and ensuring both feel comfortable discussing these topics can lead to a more satisfying connection. Some men may still choose to engage in intercourse with you, even if you're not *as fresh* as you could be. Intercourse in this condition more than likely does not result in oral sex. In other words, if you didn't wash good enough, he isn't going down there. But I will say, many men have had sex in the doggy style position and held their breath to escape the smell of her behind. But no one wants to have that conversation in public.

5 Lack of Experience

Just like women, men vary in their comfort levels and interests regarding sexual activities. If a man appears less enthusiastic about oral sex, it doesn't necessarily indicate a lack of interest in his partner. Some men may have gone through life without much experience with oral sex compared to others. This could be because they've received praise for their performance in intercourse, and he felt/she told him good penis was enough. Or they've had consecutive interactions with women who aren't huge fans of oral sex. Alternatively, they may have gone down on someone years ago with disappointing results, leading them to avoid it altogether.

6 Past Experiences Matter

Sometimes, past experiences can influence a man's willingness to engage in oral sex. It might be linked to discomfort, insecurity, or misunderstandings. Creating a safe and non-judgmental space to discuss these experiences allows couples to work together to address any challenges that arise. You must understand that what you *see* of your partner isn't all that they are. They are also the experiences they've had. Be mindful of the world they saw before you.

———

7 Remember, these discussions should happen with empathy and understanding. Sexual exploration is a shared journey that requires trust, and a willingness to learn and adapt.

8 Older men and those with erectile issues or performance anxieties often turn to oral pleasure to enhance the experience. Even if their penis can't get hard, their tongue can. They lean on this fact and become more enthusiastic about going downtown. Over time, they grow to find joy in it and may even begin to enjoy it more than the women they're pleasing.

9 I acknowledge that a <u>single woman</u> who wants more satisfying oral pleasure might easily dismiss a man who doesn't perform oral. However, in *committed* relationships where **strong bonds** have formed over time, the idea of walking

341 Know Thy Man

away can be challenging, especially when it's due merely to the absence of his tongue exploring specific areas of your body.

6 ANTI-TOY

1 Various factors can impact a man's performance in the bedroom, diminishing his sexual satisfaction for his partner. Whether its equipment issues like erectile dysfunction or a lack of sexual knowledge and experience, the outcome for any woman remains the same. Oftentimes, men seek outside help, either finding another partner to compensate for what they lack or using sexual instruments to level the playing field.

2 Sex toys can significantly enhance the bedroom experience when a man struggles to provide pleasure naturally. For some, its commonplace to incorporate toys into the bedroom even if he performs well without any issues. While toys may not replace the warmth of a man, when used correctly, they can elevate pleasure to new heights. However, many men are hesitant to embrace the use of toys.

₃ For most men, sex is ego-driven. They have sex to assert dominance and satisfy their egos' ideal of masculinity. This ideal image involves being strong and self-willed, pleasing women in bed for praise. So, in the grand theater of false manhood, where egos dominate, men often act as puppeteers. They allow the ego to lead.

₄ Using a sexual aid rather than relying solely on natural abilities can challenge the essence of some men's egos. While a man may not object to using toys on you, using them because his penis isn't working might take some adjusting to get used to. Primarily if his ego leads and he's operating from a selfish position. Regular use of toys and becoming more familiar with her body can help a man reclaim his dominance and he can find <u>new</u> *pleasure* in *pleasuring* her.

₅ A man's journey into this unfamiliar territory, freed from the anchor of his ego, questions the very *essence* of some men. Drawing them the question themselves, *"If I can't please a woman, what am I?"*

₇ SEXUAL INTELLIGENCE

₁ Sexual intelligence reflects an individual's ability to understand the details of sexuality—emotions, communication, and relationships intertwining seamlessly. It requires heightened awareness of personal desires, boundaries, and preferences, coupled with <u>compassionate consideration for others' needs</u>. Developing sexual intelligence not only enhances relationships but also creates profoundly enriching and emotionally resonant connections.

₂ Understanding your personal desires is a foundational aspect of developing sexual intelligence. It involves a deep exploration of what you truly want from sexual experiences, including your preferences, fantasies, and boundaries. This self-awareness is crucial as it allows you to navigate intimacy with greater clarity and intention. Reflecting on your needs helps in aligning your sexual experiences with your broader emotional and relational goals.

₃ Empathy plays a vital role in enriching sexual experiences. Being attuned to your partner's emotional and physical responses enhances intimacy. It's important to be attentive to their cues and to validate their feelings, creating an environment where both partners feel valued and under-stood. The same way we listen to our partners speech, there's no difference in listening to our partners body speak.

₄ Approaching intimacy with curiosity and a willingness to experiment can lead to discovering new dimensions of pleasure and connection. Trying new activities or tech-niques with your partner helps in finding what brings both of you satisfaction and deepens your shared experiences. Engaging in this exploratory process as a team not only en-hances sexual satisfaction but also reinforces your emo-tional connection. Instead of sending him on a solo journey to find better sex techniques, join him.

₅ Finally, continuous reflection and improvement are essen-tial for maintaining a fulfilling sexual relationship. Regu-larly evaluating your sexual experiences and satisfaction al-lows you to make informed adjustments and improvements. Keeping the lines of communication open and discussing your experiences helps in addressing any concerns and cre-ating ongoing growth in your intimate life. By regularly re-assessing and adapting, you ensure that your relationship re-mains dynamic and responsive to both partners' *evolving* needs. You don't know what you like until you like it.

8 MANAGING BODY INSECURITIES IN INTIMATE MOMENTS

1 Many women grapple with body insecurities shaped by society's ever-changing landscape. Despite their inherent beauty, many hold themselves to unrealistic standards. In the intimate setting of the bedroom, these insecurities can loom large, casting doubt on how they're perceived by their partners. These doubts can create mental barriers that hinder the ability to fully experience pleasure and achieve orgasm. Even if their partner never expressed dislike with their body.

2 It's crucial to realize that being present in the moment is needed to achieve climax. Remember, if your partner is engaged and aroused, it's a testament to their desire for you. If he wasn't turned on by you, he wouldn't be erect. Any changes in his physical response do not necessarily reflect your attractiveness or desirability either.

3 During intercourse, men rely on their physical senses to fully immerse themselves in the experience; sight, smell and sound particularly. However, understand that his enjoyment doesn't solely depend on physical perfection.

Your partner derives true pleasure from the connection and intimacy shared between you, not superficial attributes.

4 Many men can have <u>satisfying</u> intercourse with women who don't fit societal beauty standards; women that the world has deemed unattractive. Believing that your sagging breasts or tummy rolls prevent anything, isn't realistic. What turns a man on more than your appearance is your *nastiness* between the sheets. I've heard many women say that men are willing to sleep with *"anything,"* yet in the same breath they may feel self-conscious about their appearance while on top of him. While it's important for everyone to strive for their own standards of beauty and self-improvement, don't let these personal standards become a <u>barrier</u> to your orgasm. Embrace the moment and focus on the connection rather than worrying about your appearance. By letting go of doubt and fully engaging, you can enhance intimacy and enjoy your sexual experiences more.

"It's okay to take that shirt off, sweetheart."

₉ **THE GUILT TRIP**

₁ It's common for anyone to feel *guilty* when considering ending a relationship, due solely to dissatisfaction in the bedroom.

₂ Recognize that your self-worth extends beyond sexual satisfaction. Relationships are multifaceted, and while physical intimacy is important, it doesn't solely define the value of it. Take a moment to reflect on your overall happiness, emotional connection, and various aspects contributing to a fulfilling partnership.

₃ **ADDRESSING SEXUAL DISSATISFACTION:**

1. **START WITH APPRECIATION**:

- **Acknowledge the Positive**: Begin the conversation by highlighting aspects of the relationship that you value. This sets a positive tone and shows that you're not just focusing on the negatives.
- *Example Phrase:* "I really appreciate how supportive and caring you've been in our relationship. I want to talk about something that's been on my mind because I believe it's important for us."

2. BE SPECIFIC ABOUT CONCERNS:

- **Describe the Issue Clearly:** Share specific instances or patterns that are causing dissatisfaction. Avoid generalizations and focus on concrete examples.

- *Example Phrase:* "I've noticed that lately, I've been feeling less connected during sex. For instance, there have been times when I felt that *we* weren't fully in sync with each other's needs."

3. EXPRESS YOUR FEELINGS:

- **Share How You Feel:** Use "I" statements to express your emotions without placing blame. This helps to communicate your feelings without making your partner feel attacked.

- *Example Phrase:* "I've been feeling a bit frustrated and disconnected. I want to make sure we're both feeling fulfilled and happy in our intimate life."

4. DISCUSS YOUR NEEDS:

- **Clearly State What You Want:** Share your specific desires and needs, and invite your partner to do the same. This helps to set a clear path to improvement.

- *Example Phrase:* "I'd like us to explore new ways to connect during intimacy. For example, I think trying different types positions in different areas of the house or new techniques could be exciting for both of us."

5. ASK FOR THEIR PERSPECTIVE:

- **Invite Their Input:** Encourage your partner to share their thoughts and feelings about the current situation. This creates a collaborative approach to finding solutions.

- *Example Phrase:* "How do you feel about our sex life? Is there anything you've wanted or needed that we haven't discussed? I want us to continue to expand."

6. EXPLORE SOLUTIONS TOGETHER:

- **Suggest and Discuss Ideas:** Propose specific ideas or activities that could enhance your sexual experience together. Be open to experimenting and trying new things.

- *Example Ideas:*
1. **New Activities:** "How about we explore different types of foreplay or try a new setting to make things feel more exciting?"
2. **Sexual Health:** "We could consider reading a book or attending a workshop on improving intimacy together. I heard they make sex so much better."
3. **Playfulness:** "Let's try incorporating some playful elements, like role-playing or surprise gestures, to add a new dimension to our experiences."

7. DISCUSS FREQUENCY & EXPECTATIONS:

- **Align on Frequency:** Talk about how often you both want to engage in sexual activities and whether these expectations align with each other's desires.
- *Example Phrase:* "I think it would be helpful for us to discuss how often we want to be intimate and make sure we're both on the same page."

8. SET BOUNDARIES AND RESPECT THEM:

- **Establish Boundaries:** Clearly define what you're both comfortable with and respect each other's limits. This helps ensure that both partners feel safe and respected.

- *Example Phrase:* "Let's talk about our boundaries and make sure we're both comfortable with the things we try. It's important to me that we both feel respected and safe."

9. PLAN REGULAR CHECK-INS:

- **Schedule Follow-Up Conversations:** Regularly check in with each other about how things are going. This keeps the lines of communication open and allows for ongoing adjustments.

- *Example Phrase:* "Can we set a time to revisit this conversation in a few weeks? I want to make sure we're both feeling good about how things are progressing."

10. BE PREPARED FOR DIFFERENT OUTCOMES:

- **Accept Various Possibilities:** Understand that these discussions may lead to different outcomes, including potential changes in the relationship dynamics or direction.

- ***Example Phrase:*** "I hope we can work through this together, but I understand if we need to reassess our relationship based on what we discover."

4 I understand that this can make physical intimacy feel like a checklist task. But once the rules are in place, the game runs on autopilot.

5 These detailed ideas aim to provide a practical framework for addressing sexual dissatisfaction with your partner while building open, respectful, and constructive communication. These *example phrases* are generic in nature, but you get a sense of the direction to take. Remember, relationships involve <u>shared effort and addressing challenges together</u>. If direct communication feels difficult, couples therapy might be beneficial.

6 Finding a path forward that meets your needs is a valid and empowering decision. However, you and your partner should work as a team to find solutions that satisfy both of your needs. This collaborative approach strengthens your bond and demonstrates a mutual commitment to the relationship's well-being.

₇ Before considering a change alone, it's crucial to ensure that both partners are putting forth their best effort. Engage in open and honest conversations, explore solutions together, and actively work on improving the situation. If, after making sincere efforts, your partner is unwilling to participate or contribute to the resolution, you may then need to reevaluate your options. Introducing toys to the bed if need be.

₈ Ultimately, while it is empowering to take charge of your own happiness, the aim in a *committed relationship* is to achieve a mutual understanding and solution. Only if it becomes clear that your partner is not equally committed to resolving the issue should you consider making decisions that could lead to significant and final changes in the relationship. Nothing should keep a woman from having the orgasm she deserves.

Read Leslie's story again, what do you think she should do?

"IT'S OKAY TO TAKE THAT SHIRT OFF, SWEETHEART."

- MANUEL V. JOHNSON | LESLIE 8:4

THE BOOK OF

SARAH

THE UNEXPECTED PROTECTOR

S arah never imagined herself in this situation, standing between two men who both claimed a place in her son's life. One was his biological father, Mark, and the other, her husband, Steve. The tension between them had been brewing for months, and today it finally reached a boiling point.

Sarah met Steve a year after she and Mark separated. Mark had been a part of her life since high school, but as they grew older, their paths diverged. He was a good father when he was around, but his visits became sporadic, and his interest waned. When Steve came into their lives, he brought a sense of stability Sarah hadn't realized they were missing. From the beginning, Steve showed an unwavering commitment to both Sarah and her son, Jake. He attended school events, helped with homework, and played catch in the backyard. Jake adored him, calling him *"Dad"* more often than not, something that didn't sit well with Mark.

The incident happened on a Saturday at Jake's little league game. Steve was coaching the team, having volunteered at the start of the season. Mark showed up unexpectedly, his presence alone enough to make the air thick with unspoken words.

As the game ended, Jake ran to Steve, excitement lighting up his face. *"Did you see my catch, Dad?"* he beamed. Steve knelt down, ruffling Jake's hair. *"You were amazing out there, buddy. I'm so proud of you."*

Mark, standing a few feet away, stiffened. Sarah saw the storm brewing in his eyes. He walked over, a forced smile on his face. *"Great game, champ,"* he said, trying to reclaim his role. Jake looked between the two men, the confusion evident on his face.

"Jake, go get your things," Sarah said, trying to diffuse the situation. As he ran off, Mark turned to Steve. *"You know, it's confusing for him to call you 'Dad.' I'm his father."*

Steve stood up, his calm demeanor unwavering. *"I'm not trying to replace you, Mark. I'm here to support Jake and be there for him."*

The words were meant to be reassuring, but Mark took them as a challenge. *"Support him? By coaching his team? By letting him call you 'Dad'? You think you can just step in and take over?"*

Sarah stepped forward, placing a hand on Steve's arm, but he gently moved it away. *"I'm here because I love him, and I love Sarah. We're a family now."*

Mark's face reddened, his fists clenching. *"You have no idea what it means to be his father."*

Steve's voice remained steady, but there was a steel edge to it now. *"Maybe not, but I know what it means to be there for him."*

The tension was palpable, and for a moment, Sarah feared a physical confrontation. But then Jake reappeared, his eyes wide with worry. *"Mom, what's going on?"*

Both men turned to him, their expressions softening. *"Nothing, sweetheart,"* Sarah said quickly. *"Let's go home."*

Mark looked at Jake, then back at Steve, his anger slowly dissipating. *"We'll talk about this later,"* he muttered before walking away.

As they drove home, Jake sat quietly in the back seat, sensing the unease. Steve reached over and took Sarah's hand, his grip reassuring. *"I'm sorry,"* he said softly. *"I didn't mean to cause trouble."*

Sarah squeezed his hand back, grateful for his presence. *"You didn't. You're just being the man Jake needs."*

But as she said the words, doubt began to creep in. Was Steve really what Jake needed? Or was he just a convenient replacement for Mark? Would Jake grow up confused about who he felt his real father was?

That night, as she lay in bed, Sarah couldn't shake the feeling of uncertainty. She knew Steve loved Jake, but how much of this was driven by his desire to be a father and how much by his love for her? And what about Mark? Would he ever step up and be the father Jake needed?

The questions swirled in her mind, leaving her with a nagging sense of unease. She wanted to believe that everything would work out, but for now, she was left wondering what the future held for her, Steve, and Jake…. and mark.

₁ THE STEPFATHER

₁ When relationships end and new ones begin, we often carry remnants of our past, including our children. Entering a new relationship means committing not only to a new partner but also to the baggage they bring with them.

₂ A man who enters a new relationship with serious intent understands this. Those without serious intentions may overlook the baggage, expecting a brief relationship. However, a man with long-term intentions approaches the situation with a commitment to both his partner and her children, thus becoming a stepfather.

₃ Many stepfathers take great pride in their role.
Often family-oriented, these men cherish the idea of raising a child, imparting their wisdom, and building their own confidence through this responsibility. Their love for their partner and willingness to do anything for her also motivates them.

₄ On the other hand, some stepfathers contribute very little, only stepping in when asked and never forming a lasting bond with the child.

₂ THE 2ND DAD

₁ When the biological parents are co-parenting, the stepfather's role is different compared to when the biological father is not involved. In these situations, the stepfather often acts as a secondary dad. His main focus is on the child's interactions with *him*, *his* woman, and *his* household. While he naturally cares for the child, his parenting is limited because the biological father is actively involved and aware of everything happening in his child's life.

₂ UNDERSTANDING THE ROLE OF THE 2ND DAD

1. Primary Supporter: The stepfather's primary focus is on providing emotional support and stability within his household. While he naturally cares for the child, his parenting actions are often supplementary to those of the biological father. Acting as a Robin to the biological father's Batman.

2. Respect for Boundaries: Recognizing and respecting the boundaries set by the biological father is crucial. The stepfather's role involves ensuring that his interactions and decisions do not overstep the primary parental authority of the biological father.

3. Building Positive Relationships: The stepfather aims to build a positive and nurturing relationship with the child, which includes understanding the child's needs and interests. This relationship is based on mutual respect and affection, contributing to the child's emotional development.

4. **Household Harmony:** A significant aspect of the stepfather's role is maintaining harmony within his household. This involves balancing his relationship with his woman, the child, and managing his own expectations and contributions without causing friction with the biological father. Keeping his household harmonious.

₃ KEY RESPONSIBILITIES AND CHALLENGES

1. Emotional Stability: Providing a stable and loving environment where the child feels secure and valued. This includes participating in everyday activities, offering guidance, and being a reliable figure the child can turn to.

2. **Cooperation with Biological Father:** Collaborating with the biological father to ensure consistency in parenting approaches and decisions. This cooperation helps in presenting a united front, minimizing confusion and conflicts for the child.

3. **Navigating Loyalty Conflicts:** Children may feel torn between their loyalty to their biological father and their stepfather. The stepfather needs to navigate these feelings sensitively, ensuring the child does not feel pressured to choose sides. Making sure the child knows where their bloodline stems from.

4. Limitations in Discipline: While the stepfather can offer support and guidance, disciplinary actions are often reserved for the biological parents. This can sometimes create challenges in maintaining authority and respect within the household. But it allows the biological parent comfort in knowing their child is safe.

₄ STRATEGIES FOR SUCCESSFUL CO-PARENTING

1. Open Communication: Regular and open communication between all parties—stepfather, biological father, and partner—is essential. This ensures everyone is on the same page regarding the child's upbringing and any issues that may arise. It's okay to be adults and talk.

2. Consistency in Rules: Maintaining consistency in household rules and expectations helps provide a sense of security and structure for the child. This consistency should align with the rules of the biological father to avoid conflicts and misunderstandings.

3. **Respecting the Child's Feelings:** Acknowledging and validating the child's feelings towards both their biological father and stepfather helps in building trust and emotional security. Encouraging the child to express their emotions without fear of judgment is vital. What does the child want?

4. **Being Patient and Understanding:** Building a strong, positive relationship with the child takes time. The stepfather needs to be patient, understanding, and willing to invest the effort required to develop a meaningful bond. Move at a pace that's comfortable for the child.

5. **Creating a Team Approach:** The child needs to see that both the biological father and stepfather are working together for his or her best interest. This can significantly enhance the child's sense of security and overall well-being.

5 Remember this is all based on the biological father being 100% on board with co-parenting.

3 DADS NOT AROUND

1 A stepfather thrives when he is granted full authority as a father. This doesn't mean just in a disciplinary sense, but in all aspects of decision-making and involvement. When he is

recognized as a key figure in the child's life, he is empowered to make important decisions about education, health, and daily routines.

₂ This comprehensive involvement allows him to develop a deep, meaningful relationship with the child, bringing upon mutual respect and trust. Without the presence of another man challenging his role, he is more open and willing to fully embrace the responsibilities of being a father.

₃ When a stepfather's role is fully integrated, he becomes an essential part of the family unit. His contributions are not second-guessed or undermined by a more authoritative male figure, which allows him to act confidently and assertively in the best interests of the child. This sense of authority and respect creates a stable and nurturing environment where the child feels secure and supported.

₄ As the stepfather consistently shows up for the child, participates in important moments, and provides guidance, the child begins to see him as a true father figure. This shift is often marked by the child starting to call him *"Dad"* and the stepfather referring to the child as his son or daughter.

₅ This bond doesn't have to form solely in the absence of the biological father, but it tends to develop more quickly and more deeply when the biological father is not around. Without the presence of the biological father, there are fewer conflicts over parenting styles and fewer loyalty issues for the child to navigate. The stepfather can step into a clear and unambiguous role, which simplifies the family dynamics and allows the relationships to flourish naturally.

₆ However, even in situations where the biological father is still involved, a stepfather can establish a strong, positive relationship by working collaboratively with the biological father and ensuring that the child's needs are always the priority. This approach, although potentially more complex, can also lead to a deeply rewarding family structure where the child benefits from the love and support of multiple parental figures.

₄ IF IT WASN'T FOR YOUR MOTHER

₁ When introducing a new man into your children's lives, it's crucial to gauge his true intentions regarding your child's well-being. Does he genuinely care, or is it all an act to win you over? Many men will go to great lengths to secure the woman they desire, even using a child's innocence to gain favor.

₂ Some men will play the role of a loving father just to demonstrate husband-like qualities, hoping to win your heart. They understand that as a mother, your instinct is to seek both physical and emotional shelter for your children. By creating a false sense of security, they make you feel safe and cared for.

₃ However, while they play this role, they may be living a double life, never truly committing to the idea of a family. Their presence is only physical, with their heart and mind elsewhere.

₄ These men may have various reasons for their deception: a lack of long-term intentions, needing a place to stay, or even having another family entirely.

₅ Although they can be difficult to identify, here are three signs to watch for:

1. INCONSISTENT INVOLVEMENT:

Surface-Level Engagement: He only shows interest in the child when it's convenient or when he knows he's being watched, with interactions that lack genuine warmth.

Fluctuating Attention: His involvement is inconsistent, marked by periods of intense attention followed by detachment.

2. LACK OF INITIATIVE:

Minimal Effort: He rarely initiates activities involving the child, always waiting for you to take the lead.

Avoidance of Responsibility: He avoids meaningful tasks like helping with homework or attending school events, showing a lack of commitment to you both as a whole.

3. OVEREMPHASIS ON APPEARANCE:

Public Display vs. Private Actions: He is more affectionate in public or on social media, but distant in private.

Performative Gestures: His grand gestures lack follow-through in everyday care and support, indicating concern for appearances over genuine investment. He wants to look like a dad, not be one.

6 If he has kids, watch how he treats them. People can change, but their past doesn't. Knowing who someone is to-day, *sometimes* can be seen in the path they travelled yester-day.

5 LISTEN TO YOUR CHILD

1 This world can be harsh and cruel. I've heard many stories about stepfathers taking advantage of their stepchildren in ways we won't discuss here. The key message is to always listen to your children. Too many women bring strangers

into their homes, falling for the facade he presents. While he may show affection for you and your child, remember that he is not the child's biological father. Any perverse thoughts he has can, unfortunately, be directed towards your child. If he makes your child uncomfortable, investigate that.

2 When you start dating, it's not just about your happiness; your child's well-being is equally important. Ignoring your child's discomfort or cries for help can have serious consequences. Always prioritize their safety and trust your instincts.

3 SIX WARNING SIGNS OF INAPPROPRIATE BEHAVIOR

1. EXCESSIVE ALONE TIME:

- **Isolation**: He frequently seeks opportunities to be alone with your child without a clear or necessary reason.
- **Secretive Behavior**: He becomes secretive about his interactions with your child, avoiding discussions or explanations about their time together.

2. OVERSTEPPING BOUNDARIES:

- **Inappropriate Touching**: Physical contact that seems excessive, inappropriate, or makes your child uncomfortable.

- **Personal Space**: Invading your child's personal space in unnecessary or unwelcome ways.

3. BEHAVIORAL CHANGES IN YOUR CHILD:

- **Anxiety and Withdrawal**: Your child starts showing signs of anxiety, fear, or withdrawal when around him or when anticipating being alone with him.
- **Unexplained Changes**: Sudden changes in your child's behavior, such as becoming unusually quiet, fearful, or acting out, which can indicate discomfort or distress.

4. EXCESSIVE CONTROL:

- **Monitoring Activities**: He overly monitors or restricts your child's activities, showing undue interest in where they go and who they interact with.
- **Influence**: He tries to influence your child's decisions and behavior in ways that seem controlling or manipulative.

5. INAPPROPRIATE CONVERSATIONS:

- **Sexual Topics**: He initiates conversations with your child about sexual topics that are not age-appropriate.
- **Secrets**: Encourages your child to keep secrets from you, especially about their interactions or conversations.

6. UNUSUAL ATTENTION AND GIFTS:

- **Favoritism**: Showing an unusual amount of attention or favoritism towards your child, more than what is appropriate for the relationship.
- **Gifts and Privileges**: Frequently giving your child gifts or special privileges that seem disproportionate or aimed at gaining their trust and affection.

4 I'm not suggesting that gifts are a red flag. Just keep in mind that tragedy is often preceded by joy. Meaning, for most predators to get what they want, they have to bring joy and comfort to their victims first. Don't be blinded by that.

5 Many mothers add up all the gifts and positive acts of service he has given the child. When her child comes to tell her, *"Mr. Steve is a bad man!"* She can't process it. Her data reads the opposite, so she doesn't believe her own the child.

6 I want all mothers and fathers to register *obsessive gift giving* in their database under "Positive love" *and* "caution."

7 These signs can help you identify potential inappropriate behavior and ensure your child's safety. If you observe any of these behaviors, it is important to trust your instincts and take appropriate action to protect your child if need be. But if nothing else, just watch and be aware.

₆ THE BIOLOGICAL FATHER

₁ It's often easy to overlook or dismiss the biological father, thinking, "If he cared, he would be here." However, he is an integral part of your child's DNA. Regardless of any resentment *you* may hold, your child may not share your feelings, and even if they do now, they may change their perspective of their father as they grow older. Therefore, the well-being of the biological father matters to some degree.

BIO-HARZARD DAD

₂ In the present situation, where does the biological father fit into all of this? His role largely depends on his maturity level and his feelings about you and the new man in your life.

₃ Some men, upon seeing you thrive with someone else, realize that they might have been the problem all along and want their family back. On the other hand, some biological fathers may go out of their way to make your life difficult, trying to create chaos in your household to mirror their own turmoil inside. These men often feel the need to assert dominance in this complex dynamic, attempting to scare the new man away. Some new boyfriends may leave, deciding that the baggage is not worth it, while others may stay, feeling they have something to prove as well. This often leads to conflicts and even worse outcomes.

4 It takes maturity to let go of these grievances and address issues like adults. Boys fight their problems out; fighting is essentially an adult temper tantrum. Men, however, talk their problems out. If you find yourself in this scenario, you may need to question your choice of individuals. Unfortunately, some women are attracted to this toxic behavior, letting ego and conflict dictate their relationships. If your man prefers to fight or shoot before having a calm lengthy conversation, you not only put your child in danger, but this could be an indication of how he'll treat you when his emotions run high.

5 Additionally, when the relationship ended due to something you may have caused, some biological fathers can't get over it. They become angry at the idea of you moving on happily without facing what they perceive as your deserved karma. In turn, they try to become that karma in the flesh, making your life difficult as a form of retribution.

BIO-LOGICAL DAD

6 First you have the biological fathers who are solely focused on their role as a parent. They live their lives independently and only communicate when it concerns their child. They

don't interfere with your relationship unless their son or daughter is directly affected. These men make co-parenting easy by being mature and managing their own lives. They respect the decisions made in each household—his primary concern is what happens under his roof, while respecting your autonomy in your home. His phone is always available for important calls, but he doesn't necessarily check in daily.

7 These fathers may or may not care for your new partner, but as long as the new man's actions don't negatively impact their child, they remain at ease. They might want to meet the new partner to get a sense of who will be around their son or daughter, especially if they feel their child is vulnerable.

8 Then there are assertive biological fathers. These men include you and your new partner in activities, parties, and family trips. They do this partly because they are outgoing, but also to maintain a sense of oversight on the situation. It's also a subtle way to show that they are livelier and more adventurous, quietly comparing themselves to your new partner.

9 These fathers want to be involved in every aspect of their child's life, including decisions made in *your* household. They strive to be informed and part of the decision-making process, which can sometimes cause friction. However, their intentions are generally aimed at the well-being and

progression of the child, rather than disrupting your relationship.

₇ **FATHERS**

₁ In the end, stepfathers can be a true blessing when the role is embraced and executed with care. It can be challenging for them, especially if they have their own children living elsewhere. The emotional strain can be significant, not only for him but also because the mother of his biological child may resent his commitment to your child, potentially straining his own parent-child relationship. His kids mother may go as far as trying to keep his child from him due to the relationship he's formed with yours.

₂ For men who have never had children, becoming a stepfather offers them a unique opportunity to step into a fatherly role without the full commitment of having a biological child. For those who cannot have children, this experience can feel like a second chance, a precious opportunity to fulfill a deeply held desire to nurture and guide a young life.

₃ When choosing a stepfather for your child, remember that the decision is yours. It's important to look beyond superficial qualities like wealth or looks. Consider whether this man embodies the values and lifestyle you would want your son to emulate. After all, living under the same roof, your child is likely to absorb and reflect his influence. Choose wisely, ensuring that your partner not only loves you but is also a positive role model for your child.

4 Fatherhood is a divine gift, a sacred trust given to those chosen to guide the next generation. While some men may squander this priceless opportunity, there are others who rise to the challenge, wearing the mantle of fatherhood with pride and honor. To stand among those who have the privilege to shape the future is not just a blessing, but a profound duty.

5 To the fathers who embrace this responsibility, who pour their wisdom and love into the hearts of their children, we salute you. Your dedication and sacrifice illuminate the path for the generations to come. You are the unsung heroes, the silent warriors, who mold the future with every act of love and guidance.

6 And to those who recognize their own unreadiness, who understand that they are not yet prepared to bear this immense responsibility, we extend our prayers. May you find the strength and wisdom to grow, to one day take up the shield of fatherhood with the honor it deserves.

₇ Let us celebrate those who understand that fatherhood is not just a role, but a legacy. For it is your love, and your unwavering commitment that the world becomes a better place.

Read Sarah's story again, what do you think she's dealing with?

"...SOME BIOLOGICAL FATHERS MAY GO OUT OF THEIR WAY TO MAKE YOUR LIFE DIFFICULT, TRYING TO CREATE CHAOS IN YOUR HOUSEHOLD TO MIRROR THEIR OWN TURMOIL INSIDE"

- MANUEL V. JOHNSON | SARAH 6:3

THE BOOK OF

MARY

LOVE'S FINAL JOURNEY

Mary and Willard had been married for 45 years, a union that had weathered the storms of life and emerged stronger. Their love story was one of companionship, shared dreams, and countless cherished moments. They had built a life together, raising children, celebrating milestones, and supporting each other through thick and thin.

One afternoon, they visited the hospital for what they thought would be a routine check-up. The atmosphere in the waiting room was filled with the soft hum of conversations and the occasional clinking of medical instruments. Mary held Willard's hand tightly, her thumb gently caressing his knuckles in a reassuring gesture. Despite the ordinary setting, an unspoken tension lingered in the air.

When the doctor finally called them in, they exchanged a hopeful glance before following him into a small, sterile room. The doctor's face was serious, and Mary's heart began to race. She felt a tightening in her chest as he began to speak, his words carefully measured but heavy with significance.

"Willard, I'm afraid we have some difficult news. The tests show that you have cancer."

The words hit Mary like a bolt of lightning, shattering the peaceful existence they had known. She watched as Willard's face went cold, his eyes wide with shock and fear. The lost look in his gaze mirrored the turmoil now raging inside of her. Mary, who had always been a pillar of strength, felt a wave of vulnerability wash over her. She reached for Willard's hand, gripping it as if to anchor them both against the storm that had suddenly engulfed their lives.

The drive home was silent, each of them lost in their own thoughts. Mary's mind raced through memories of their life together—the laughter, the tears, the quiet moments of simple joy. How had they gone from those cherished times to this heartbreaking reality? She glanced at Willard, who stared blankly out the window, his usual calm demeanor replaced by a noticeable sense of despair.

At home, Mary busied herself with making tea, her hands trembling as she set the kettle on the stove. Willard sat at the kitchen table, his head in his hands. The sight of him so broken, so lost, made her heart ache. She wanted to say something, to comfort him, but words failed her.

As the days passed, the reality of their situation began to sink in. Willard's health began to deteriorate, and Mary found herself thrust into the role of caregiver. Each day brought new challenges, each one more daunting than the last. The *physical* toll of caring for Willard was immense, but it was the *emotional* strain that weighed heaviest on her heart.

Mary felt a deep sadness as she watched the man she loved most in the world struggle with pain and fear. The lost look in his eyes became a constant reminder of their shared anguish. She battled with feelings of helplessness, unable to shield Willard from the relentless progression of his illness.

She often found herself sitting alone in their bedroom, staring at the photographs that lined the dresser. Pictures of happier times—family vacations, anniversaries, the birth of their children. Each image a sharp contrast to the present reality. The sight of other women with their healthy husbands stirred a mix of emotions within her. A sense of unfairness along with growing anger of the seemingly cruel circumstances ate at her thoughts.

Mary's faith, which had been her bedrock for so long, faced its own trial. She struggled to reconcile her belief in a loving, all-powerful God with the suffering that Willard was enduring. In her darkest moments, she found herself questioning everything she had held dear. Yet, despite her doubts, she clung to the enduring love she and Willard shared, finding comfort in their unbreakable bond. But as Willard's condition worsened, Mary prepared herself for the inevitable. The thought of life without him was almost unbearable, but she knew she had to be strong.

When Willard finally transitioned and passed away, Mary felt an overwhelming sense of loss, a void that no amount of time could ever truly fill.

In the months that followed, Mary faced the daunting task of rebuilding her life. The grief was a constant companion, but so were the memories of a love that had stood the test of time. As she navigated the uncertain terrain of widowhood, she drew strength from the lessons learned during their 45 years together.

1 **MY DEAREST**

1 I can't fathom the depth of emotions you're navigating as you confront the harsh realities of your husband's illness. In these incredibly challenging times, your feelings matter, and I want you to know that your pain is seen and acknowledged.

2 The conversations with your husband about his condition may bring about unwanted emotions, but they are a lifeline for both of you. Sharing your innermost feelings, fears, and hopes helps strengthen your connection during these times. Your vulnerability is a testament to the strength of your bond.

3 Practical decisions about your husband's health and end-of-life plans are daunting, and it's okay to feel overwhelmed. The talks, though emotionally draining, are essential for clarity and preparation. Your support network, comprising of family, friends, and caregivers, is a solid base. Lean on them, allowing yourself moments for self-care. Prioritize your well-being; consider therapy, engage in activities that bring joy, and ensure you get the rest you desperately need.

4 Dealing with changed roles and responsibilities is an emotional tightrope. Discussing these changes openly with your husband ensures a shared understanding, easing

the burden on both of you. Your adaptability is a testament to your resilience and faith.

₅ Grief, my dear, is a heavy companion on this journey. Allow yourself the space to acknowledge and process your emotions. Seek comfort in counseling or support groups, where your pain can be met with empathy and understanding. Finding others in your shoes will help you feel seen.

₆ In the midst of the challenges, find moments of joy and connection. Cherish memories, create new ones, and celebrate the beautiful bond you share. Engage in activities that bring comfort and peace, whether it's sharing quiet moments or pursuing personal hobbies.

₇ Please remember, you're not alone in this. Your strength and resilience are awe-inspiring. Embrace the support surrounding you, keep those lines of communication open, and continue prioritizing your well-being. Through your efforts, you're creating a haven of compassion and support for your husband in his most vulnerable moments. He needs that now more than ever. The more at peace you are, the increased quality of his last days become.

2 LIFE AFTER DEATH FOR *HER*

1 After losing her significant other to an illness, the following months or even years can feel like riding an emotional rollercoaster. Initially, it feels like a bad dream—everything is turned upside down, and the pain is overwhelming.

2 Soon after, there's a mix of feeling lost, angry, and sometimes just numb. The daily routines they shared are gone, leaving an empty space that's hard to fill.

3 As time progresses, dealing with the grief becomes like piecing together a puzzle. Some days are manageable, while others are tough, triggered by a scent, a memory, or a meaningful date. Part of the journey involves rediscovering who she is without her partner, which can be a challenging process. Coping requires finding ways to manage—talking to friends and family or seeking help from a therapist. The path to healing isn't straightforward.

4 Over time, the pain may become *less intense*, and memories of her loved one may transform into a source of comfort rather than sorrow. When times do become challenging, the thought of his laughter can now bring her to a smile.

5 She begins to discover a new version of herself. Engaging in activities that bring comfort, staying close to loved ones, and trying new things all play a role. It's a journey of learning to carry her partner's memory while building a new life.

6 Support from friends, family, and new connections can be incredibly helpful. Sharing laughter and tears with others makes the tough times a bit easier. Eventually, she might find a <u>new sense of purpose</u>—living a life that honors the love she had.

7 As the days goes by, the pain doesn't disappear, but it changes. It becomes part of her story, a connection to her late partner. This journey is undeniably tough, but it offers opportunities for personal growth and finding a new kind of *normal*.

8 SIX ACTIVITIES TO CONSIDER AFTER THE LOSS OF A LIFE PARTNER

1. Support Groups

Many widows find peace in joining support groups where they can <u>connect with others</u> who have experienced a similar loss. Sharing experiences, emotions, and coping strategies provides a sense of understanding and community. If local support groups are unavailable, consider online communities or specialized books for valuable support and insights.

2. Hobbies and Creative Outlets

Engaging in hobbies or creative pursuits helps channel emotions and find joy amidst grief. Whether it's painting, writing, gardening, or any other activity, these pursuits offer a positive outlet for self-expression. Even if these activities are new to you, giving them a try might reveal a new version of yourself.

3. Volunteer Work

Some widows find fulfillment in giving back to their communities through volunteer work. Helping others can provide a sense of purpose and connection, positively impacting the lives of those in need.

4. Educational Pursuits

Pursuing further education or learning new skills can be a path for personal growth. Taking classes, attending workshops, or even going back to school can open new interests and expand horizons.

5. Traveling

Exploring new places and experiencing different cultures can be rejuvenating and empowering. Traveling provides a break from routine, a chance to create new memories, and an opportunity for self-discovery. It's not about replacing old memories but adding new ones, allowing the mind to rest and explore new thoughts.

6. **Fitness and Wellness Activities**
Engaging in physical activities, such as yoga, walking groups, or fitness classes, contributes to overall well-being and provides a social outlet. Connecting with others who share similar health and wellness goals can build a supportive community around you.

3 **HOW DOES *HE* FEEL**

1 As a man faces the reality of his impending death, a wave of emotions, fears, and concerns can flood his thoughts. One common fear is the thought of leaving his beloved wife alone. Worrying about her well-being, both emotionally and practically, weighs heavily on his heart. This is why your strength is so important for him to see. Your resilience brings him peace, knowing you can handle life without him, even if *you* feel uncertain.

2 He may also worry about you moving on with another man. The thought of someone else walking through his home can deeply stir his emotions. Although he knows he can't prevent you from finding happiness again, he

wishes to be the last man you share your life with. True love, however, means wanting you to be happy, even if it's not with him and in *his* last days *your* happiness matters.

₃ Thoughts about his legacy also arise. He wonders if he fulfilled his purpose—did he make the most of his time? He reflects on the impact he had on his family, friends, and the world. He questions whether he imparted enough wisdom, love, and guidance to his children to help them navigate life's challenges. The desire to be remembered as a good husband, father, and man of integrity occupies his thoughts, seeking reassurance that his presence will linger in the hearts of those he leaves behind. It's partly your job to assure him of this.

₄ The prospect of missing significant moments in his children's lives is a source of deep sorrow. Graduations, weddings, and everyday joys he won't be there to share add layers to his grief.

₅ If he has spiritual beliefs, fear of the unknown afterlife may also stir deep contemplation. The uncertainty of what lies beyond can evoke mixed emotions, from anxiety to seeking comfort in faith. Leaning on spiritual beliefs can provide some peace and make his transition easier. The hope of seeing loved ones again can be comforting.

₆ Amongst these fears and worries, a dying husband may find calm in cherishing the moments he has left with loved ones. Expressing love, imparting final words of wisdom, and creating lasting memories become precious endeavors. His concerns may also extend to ensuring his affairs are in order, easing the burden on his family. Making sure life insurance policies and other financial arrangements are in place.

₇ It's a complex emotional landscape during his final days, encompassing love, regret, fear, and acceptance. Each person's experience is unique, reflecting the deeply personal nature of meeting the mortality in which we all face. We all go at some point.

₈ The **six points** below collectively contribute to a more positive and meaningful experience, creating an environment of love, connection, and fulfillment during his final days.

1. Quality Time with Loved Ones
Spending meaningful moments with family and friends can bring great positivity to his life. Creating new memories, sharing laughter, and feeling the warmth of companionship contribute to a sense of love and connection.

2. Expression of Love and Affection

Honest expressions of love and affection from those close to him can uplift his spirits. Verbalizing feelings, reminiscing about shared experiences, and affirming the <u>impact</u> he has had on others provide a profound sense of validation and comfort.

3. Comfort and Support

Providing physical and emotional comfort is crucial. Ensure that he is surrounded by a supportive and caring environment, with attention to pain management and emotional well-being.

4. Fulfillment of Wishes and Bucket List Items

Assisting in the fulfillment of any remaining wishes or helping him achieve items on his bucket list can bring a sense of accomplishment and joy. It allows him to experience moments of fulfillment and satisfaction during his remaining time.

5. Spiritual or Emotional Guidance

For those with spiritual beliefs, connecting with religious or spiritual leaders can provide comfort and guidance. Making things right with God allows for an assured resting after the shedding of this worldly body. Emotional support from counselors or therapists can also help navigate complex feelings, offering a space for reflection and expression.

6. Legacy Projects

Engaging in projects that contribute to the creation of a lasting legacy can bring positivity. This might involve recording messages, videos to future generations packed with valuable lessons or creating keepsakes for loved ones, can give him a sense of permanence.

₄ LIFE'S LAST STOP

₁ In the twilight of our lives, when the final chapters are being written, what we truly yearn for is to be heard, to be seen, and to be remembered as someone who left a mark on this world. Our actions and the impacts we make often define the narrative of our existence, especially as the sands of time slip away and each moment becomes infinitely precious. As the clock ticks, the realization dawns upon us that our true legacy lies in the relationships we have nurtured and the love we have shared.

₂ An old proverb says, *"A tree is known by its fruit."* This simple yet profound truth captures the essence of our lives. The fruits of our actions, the love we give, and the memories we create are the enduring legacies that outlive us.

₃ As we reflect on our journey, we discover that life was never about the material accomplishments or the brief moments of personal glory. It was always about the connections we forged, the hands we held, and the hearts we touched. It is in the quiet moments of shared laughter, the comfort of a loving embrace, and the unspoken understanding between souls that we find the true meaning of our existence.

₄ As we face the inevitable end, we realize that the value of our lives is measured not by the scope of our achievements but by the depth of our relationships. We come to understand that our greatest gift to the world is the love we have given and the memories we leave behind.

₅ In the end, we all seek the same thing: to know that we <u>mattered</u>, that we made a <u>difference</u>, and that our presence on this earth was <u>felt</u> and <u>cherished</u>. It is in this realization that we find peace, knowing that our lives were not lived in vain, but were a testament to the power of love and connection.

₆ So, as we prepare to turn the final page, let us remember that our legacy is woven into the hearts of those we loved. For it is through them that our story continues, and it is in their memories that we achieve immortality. Our lives, like the tree's fruit, will nourish and inspire long after we are gone.

7 As time becomes ever more precious, let us prioritize the relationships that define us, for it is through these bonds that we truly understand that life was never about us alone, but about the love we shared with others. And in this love, we find our eternal legacy.

KNOW THY MAN
The End

"...OUR GREATEST GIFT TO THE WORLD IS THE LOVE WE HAVE GIVEN AND THE MEMORIES WE LEAVE BEHIND."

- MANUEL V. JOHNSON | MARY 4:4

KNOW
THY
MAN

**A DEEPER DIVE INTO YOUR
MANS MIND**

The Male Psyche

INTRODUCTION TO MALE PSYCHOLOGY

Understanding male psychology is crucial for improving relationships and creating deeper connections. Men and women often approach relationships with different perspectives, influenced by a combination of biological, evolutionary, and societal factors. By delving into these aspects, we can gain valuable insights into why men behave the way they do and how these behaviors impact their relationships. This foundational knowledge serves as a crucial stepping stone for anyone seeking to navigate and enhance their interactions with men.

The importance of understanding male psychology extends beyond mere curiosity; it is about creating empathy and effective communication. When we comprehend the underlying reasons behind men's actions and reactions, we are better equipped to build stronger, more meaningful connections.

BIOLOGICAL AND EVOLUTIONARY FACTORS

Biological influences, such as genetics and brain chemistry, play a significant role in shaping male behavior. Research has shown that there are notable differences between male and female brain structures, affecting everything from emotional processing to decision-making (See Appendix H for more details). For instance, areas of the brain associated with spatial awareness and motor control tend to be more developed in men, while regions related to emotional regulation and communication are often more pronounced in women. Understanding these differences can help explain why men might approach problems differently or express emotions in unique ways.

Evolutionary psychology further illuminates male behavior by examining how ancient survival mechanisms influence modern actions. Traits such as competitiveness, risk-taking, and the desire to protect and provide are deeply rooted in evolutionary history. These traits were essential for survival in early human societies and continue to manifest in contemporary behaviors. Recognizing these evolutionary influences helps us understand why certain patterns persist and how they can affect relationship dynamics today.

SOCIETAL EXPECTATIONS AND CONDITIONING

Societal norms and expectations have a profound impact on male behavior. From a young age, boys are often conditioned to adhere to traditional notions of masculinity, which emphasize traits like stoicism, assertiveness, and self-reliance. These societal pressures can lead men to suppress their emotions, avoid vulnerability, and conform to rigid gender roles. The influence of media, cultural narratives, and peer groups further reinforces these expectations, shaping how men perceive themselves and interact with others.

Cultural background also plays a crucial role in shaping male psychology. Different cultures have varied expectations and norms regarding male behavior, which can influence men's attitudes and actions in relationships. For example, in some cultures, men are encouraged to be dominant and authoritative, while in others, they may be expected to be nurturing and collaborative.

COMMON TRAITS AND CHARACTERISTICS

Typical male traits such as competitiveness, problem-solving approaches, and risk-taking are often evident in various aspects of life, including relationships. Competitiveness can manifest as a drive to succeed and excel, which can be beneficial in achieving personal and professional goals. However, it can also lead to conflicts if not balanced with cooperation and compromise. Similarly, men's tendency to approach problems with a solution-oriented mindset can be advantageous in resolving issues but may sometimes come across as dismissive of emotional needs.

Recognizing the strengths and weaknesses of these traits is essential for navigating relationship dynamics effectively. While competitiveness and problem-solving skills can bring positive contributions to a partnership, it is crucial to balance them with empathy and emotional intelligence.

PRACTICAL APPLICATIONS

Applying the knowledge gained from understanding male psychology can significantly improve communication and relationship satisfaction. One practical approach is to engage in activities and exercises designed to create better mutual understanding. For example, couples can participate in active listening exercises, where each partner takes turns speaking and listening without interruption, ensuring that both feel heard and valued.

Additionally, practicing empathy by putting oneself in the other's shoes can enhance emotional connection and reduce misunderstandings.

Reflecting on personal experiences and considering how these insights apply to your relationships can also be highly beneficial. Take time to observe and analyze interactions, noting how biological, evolutionary, and societal influences might be at play. Use these reflections to guide your interactions and expectations, creating a more compassionate and informed approach to your relationship.

SUMMARY AND CONCLUSION

In summary, understanding male psychology involves recognizing the interplay of biological, evolutionary, and societal influences on men's behavior. This foundational knowledge is crucial for improving relationships and creating deeper connections. By exploring the typical traits and characteristics of men, we gain valuable insights into their strengths and challenges, allowing us to navigate relationship dynamics more effectively.

APPENDIX

APPENDIX A

1. Confirmation Bias Definition:

Confirmation bias is a cognitive bias that involves favoring information that confirms one's preexisting beliefs or hypotheses while disregarding or minimizing information that contradicts them. This bias can significantly influence various aspects of decision-making and perception, often leading to flawed judgments and conclusions.

Here's a detailed look at confirmation bias:

Securely_attached individuals generally maintain a steady view of their partners, seeing both good and bad traits without major shifts in perception. This balanced perspective helps them handle relationship dynamics more smoothly.

Anxiously attached individuals might initially idealize their partners to feel secure. But as they start noticing flaws, their anxiety and insecurity increase, causing conflicts.

Avoidantly attached people might ignore negative traits at first to keep their sense of independence. Over time, when these traits become too obvious, they may distance themselves emotionally, which can also create problems in the relationship.

2. Key Characteristics

1. **Selective Attention**: Individuals tend to pay more attention to information that supports their existing beliefs and ignore or downplay information that challenges them.
2. **Selective Recall**: People are more likely to remember details that confirm their beliefs and forget information that contradicts them.

3. **Interpretation Bias**: The same piece of evidence can be interpreted in different ways depending on one's preconceptions. People tend to interpret ambiguous information as supporting their existing attitudes.

3. Examples

- **Media Consumption**: People often choose news sources that align with their political or social beliefs, reinforcing their existing views.
- **Scientific Research**: Researchers might favor data that supports their hypothesis and overlook data that doesn't.
- **Personal Relationships**: If someone believes a friend is kind, they may overlook instances of rudeness and focus on acts of kindness.

4. Impact

1. **Decision-Making**: Confirmation bias can lead to poor decisions because it prevents individuals from considering all relevant information.
2. **Perpetuation of Stereotypes**: It can reinforce stereotypes and prejudices, as people focus on behavior that confirms their biases about a group and ignore behavior that doesn't.
3. **Conflict and Misunderstanding**: In personal and professional relationships, confirmation bias can cause misunderstandings and conflicts, as individuals are not open to alternative viewpoints.

5. Mitigation Strategies

1. **Awareness and Education**: Understanding that confirmation bias exists is the first step towards mitigating its effects.

2. **Seeking Disconfirming Evidence**: Actively look for information that challenges your beliefs.

3. **Consider Alternative Explanations**: Try to think of multiple reasons for why something might be true or false.

4. **Critical Thinking and Skepticism**: Question the validity of your own assumptions and the information you encounter.

5. **Diverse Perspectives**: Engage with a variety of viewpoints and sources of information to broaden your understanding.

6. In Research

In scientific research, confirmation bias can compromise the integrity of studies. To counter this, researchers use blind and double-blind study designs, peer review, and replication to ensure that findings are robust and not influenced by the researchers' biases.

Sources
- Encyclopaedia Britannica. *"Confirmation Bias."* Retrieved from Encyclopaedia Britannica.
- Cherry, Kendra. *"Confirmation Bias: How to Identify and Overcome It."* Verywell Mind. Retrieved from Verywell Mind.
- The Decision Lab. *"Confirmation Bias."* Retrieved from The Decision Lab.

APPENDIX B

1. Attachment Theory Definition:

Developed by John Bowlby and further expanded by Mary Ainsworth, Attachment Theory is a psychological model that describes the dynamics of long-term interpersonal relationships between humans. It posits that the bonds formed between children and their primary caregivers have a profound impact on an individual's emotional development and future relationships. These early attachments influence one's ability to form stable relationships throughout life by shaping expectations and behaviors in interpersonal interactions.

2. Attachment Styles:

Secure Attachment:
- **Characteristics**: Individuals feel confident and comfortable in their relationships, able to depend on others and have others depend on them. They typically have high self-esteem and are able to balance intimacy and independence.
- **Development**: Arises from consistent and responsive nurturing during childhood.
- **Impact on Relationships**: They maintain a balanced view of their partners, recognizing both positive and negative traits without significant shifts in perception.

Anxious (Preoccupied) Attachment:
- **Characteristics**: Individuals are often insecure about their relationships, seeking constant reassurance and fearing abandonment. They may appear needy or clingy.
- **Development**: Results from inconsistent nurturing, where the caregiver's availability is unpredictable.
- **Impact on Relationships**: They might initially idealize their partners but later experience heightened anxiety and insecurity as they become more aware of flaws.

Avoidant (Dismissive) Attachment:
- **Characteristics**: Individuals maintain emotional distance from others and prioritize independence over intimacy. They may appear self-sufficient and uncomfortable with closeness.
- **Development**: Emerges from nurturing that is emotionally distant or unresponsive.

- **Impact on Relationships**: They might initially ignore negative traits to maintain independence but eventually seek emotional distance when those traits become unavoidable.

Disorganized (Fearful-Avoidant) Attachment:
- **Characteristics**: Individuals display a mix of behaviors, often feeling confused or conflicted about relationships. They desire closeness but also fear it, leading to unpredictable and often tumultuous interactions.
- **Development**: Often linked to trauma or severe inconsistency in caregiving, including abuse or neglect.
- **Impact on Relationships**: They struggle with emotional regulation and often find themselves in dramatic, unstable relationships.

Sources:
Berkeley Well-Being Institute: Attachment Theory:
History, Research, & Psychology
Psychology Today:
Your Attachment Style Can Help or Harm Your Relationships

APPENDIX C

The concept that *"a man enjoys driving the car but doesn't appreciate being criticized for choosing a particular route"* also serves as a metaphor for relationships and communication dynamics between men and women. It highlights the importance of respectful and supportive communication, especially when addressing potential conflicts or disagreements. Here's an elaboration on this idea:

Respectful Communication
In any relationship, the way partners communicate with each other greatly impacts the relationship's health and stability. When a man is metaphorically "driving the car," he is in a

position of making decisions or leading in a certain area. Criticizing his decisions directly can be seen as undermining his efforts and judgment. This can lead to feelings of frustration, defensiveness, and conflict.

Constructive Feedback

The key to providing feedback in a way that maintains respect and harmony is to be constructive rather than critical. For example, instead of saying, "OMG, you're going the wrong way!" which comes off as accusatory and disrespectful, you can frame your concern in a supportive and inquisitive manner: "Is this the quickest route? I ask because..." This approach:

- Shows respect for his decision-making.
- Opens a dialogue rather than starting an argument.
- Provides an opportunity for him to explain his choice.
- Keeps the tone positive and collaborative.

Feminine Influence

The phrase *"the best way to challenge his masculinity is with your femininity"* suggests that using qualities traditionally associated with femininity—such as empathy, tactfulness, and gentleness—can be more effective in influencing or challenging a man's decisions than direct confrontation or criticism.

This approach:

- Leverages emotional intelligence to navigate conflicts.
- Encourages mutual respect and understanding.
- Avoids triggering defensiveness, creating a cooperative atmosphere.

Practical Application

In practical terms, here are a few ways to apply this concept in a relationship:

    a. **Express Concerns Tactfully**: When you have concerns or suggestions, express them in a way that shows you value his input and judgment. Use "I" statements and gentle questions to open the conversation.

b. **Acknowledge His Efforts**: Recognize and appreciate his efforts and decisions, even if you see room for improvement. Positive reinforcement can encourage more open communication.

c. **Collaborate on Solutions**: Instead of presenting an alternative as a correction, present it as a collaborative solution. For instance, "What do you think about trying this route? I heard it might be quicker."

d. **Embrace Your Femininity**: Use qualities like empathy, patience, and understanding to create a supportive environment where both partners feel valued and respected.

Benefits of This Approach

- **Strengthens Relationship**: Respectful and supportive communication strengthens the emotional bond and trust between partners.
- **Reduces Conflict**: By avoiding direct criticism, you reduce the likelihood of conflict and defensiveness.
- **Enhances Cooperation**: A collaborative approach creates a sense of teamwork and mutual respect.
- **Promotes Growth**: Constructive feedback helps both partners grow and improve without feeling attacked or devalued.

Using femininity—characterized by empathy, tact, and support—to challenge masculinity can lead to more positive interactions and a healthier, more respectful relationship dynamic. Keep in mind that these are merely suggestions, not instructions. Every relationship is different.

APPENDIX D

1. The Power of Energy and Attraction

The idea that energy attracts certain people is rooted in the concept that like attracts like. When you radiate positivity, confidence, and self-worth, you naturally draw people who resonate with those same qualities. This phenomenon suggests that our thoughts and emotions create a magnetic field that influences the kind of people and experiences we draw into our lives.

Vibrating at a Higher Frequency

When you take the time to heal and nurture yourself, you begin to vibrate at a higher frequency. This higher vibration manifests as a sense of well-being, self-assurance, and inner peace. People are naturally drawn to this positive energy. They may not always be able to articulate why they are attracted to you, but they feel the pull of your elevated vibration.

Energy and Relationships

In relationships, this energy dynamic plays a crucial role. If you are in a state of negativity or self-doubt, you might attract partners who reinforce those feelings, leading to unhealthy or unfulfilling relationships. Conversely, when you vibrate at a higher frequency, you attract partners who appreciate your worth, share your positive outlook, and contribute to your growth and happiness.

2. Self-Love Activities

To cultivate this high-vibration energy, engaging in self-love activities is essential. These activities not only promote healing but also reinforce your self-worth and happiness.

Mindfulness and Meditation

Practicing mindfulness and meditation helps center your thoughts and emotions, reducing stress and enhancing your sense of inner peace. This practice allows you to connect with your true self and creates a deep sense of self-awareness.

Physical Exercise
Regular physical exercise boosts your mood and energy levels. It also helps build self-confidence as you take care of your body and witness its strength and resilience.

Pursuing Passions
Engaging in activities that you are passionate about brings joy and fulfillment. Whether it's painting, writing, dancing, or any other hobby, immersing yourself in something you love helps you reconnect with your innermost desires and talents.

Positive Affirmations
Incorporating positive affirmations into your daily routine can shift your mindset. Repeating affirmations like "I am worthy of love and happiness" or "I am confident and strong" reinforces a positive self-image.

Setting Boundaries
Learning to set healthy boundaries is a crucial aspect of self-love. It involves recognizing your limits and protecting your emotional and mental well-being by saying no to situations or people that drain your energy.

Self-Care Rituals
Simple self-care rituals, such as taking relaxing baths, practicing skincare routines, or spending time in nature, can have a profound impact on your mental and emotional state. These rituals remind you to prioritize your well-being.

3. The Ripple Effect
As you engage in these self-love activities and elevate your energy, you create a ripple effect. The positivity you cultivate within yourself extends outward, influencing the people you

interact with and the environments you inhabit. Your higher vibration becomes a beacon, attracting like-minded individuals who appreciate and resonate with your energy.

In essence, the journey of self-love and healing transforms you into a magnet for positive experiences and relationships. By valuing and nurturing yourself, you not only enhance your own life but also inspire and uplift those around you.

Sources:
1. *"The Law of Attraction: The Basics of the Teachings of Abraham"* by Esther and Jerry Hicks
2. *"The Power of Now: A Guide to Spiritual Enlightenment*" by Eckhart Tolle
3. *"You Can Heal Your Life*" by Louise Hay
4. *"Radical Acceptance: Embracing Your Life with the Heart of a Buddha"* by Tara Brach
5. *"The Gifts of Imperfection: Let Go of Who You Think You're Supposed to Be and Embrace Who You Are"* by Brené Brown
6. *"Awaken the Giant Within: How to Take Immediate Control of Your Mental, Emotional, Physical and Financial Destiny!"* by Tony Robbins
7. Research articles from psychology journals:
   - Articles on the effects of positive affirmations and self-talk on mental health.
   - Studies on the impact of mindfulness meditation on stress reduction and emotional well-being.
8. Scientific American and Psychology Today (for articles on the science of attraction, energy, and the psychological benefits of self-love and mindfulness practices).

APPENDIX E (not a recognized diagnosis)
1. Maternal Protagonism

Definition:
Maternal Protagonism is a behavioral and psychological concept describing a woman who assumes a nurturing and leading role within her relationship. This term captures the dual nature of nurturing and leadership that such a woman exhibits, often

taking on motherly duties for her partner while providing guidance, support, and emotional sustenance.

2. Characteristics of Maternal Protagonism:

1. Nurturing Leadership:
- A Maternal Protagonist naturally takes the lead in managing both emotional and practical aspects of the relationship.
- She provides care and support, ensuring the well-being of her partner.
- Her leadership is characterized by empathy, compassion, and a protective instinct.

2. Willing Embrace:
- She willingly embraces her role, finding satisfaction in the act of nurturing and leading.
- Her actions are driven by a deep-seated desire to care for and support her partner.

3. Conditional Satisfaction:
- The Maternal Protagonist enjoys her role as long as she feels appreciated and valued.
- Her sense of fulfillment is contingent upon not feeling taken for granted or used.
- If her efforts are not reciprocated or acknowledged, she may experience distress or dissatisfaction.

4. Origins of Behavior:
- This behavior can stem from various psychological and social factors, including childhood experiences and cultural expectations.
- Women who have experienced nurturing roles in their family of origin or have been conditioned to prioritize caregiving may be more likely to exhibit Maternal Protagonism.

- Some women may develop Maternal Protagonism due to a fear of abandonment. Having been left or neglected as a child, they seek to control their partner to reduce the likelihood of being abandoned again.

5. **Impact on Relationships**:
   - Maternal Protagonism can contribute to a balanced and harmonious relationship when both partners appreciate and reciprocate the care and leadership provided.
   - However, if the dynamic becomes one-sided, with the Maternal Protagonist feeling exploited, it can lead to resentment and conflict.
   - Often, these women are unaware of the lack of leadership in their partner because they are so focused on their own contribution to the relationship.

3. Potential Diagnosis:

How one would potentially diagnose Maternal Protagonism, observe the following traits:
   - The individual naturally assumes a nurturing and leading role in the relationship.
   - She combines nurturing with leadership, providing guidance, support, and emotional sustenance.
   - She embraces this role willingly and enjoys it, driven by a desire to nurture and lead.
   - Her satisfaction depends on feeling appreciated and not taken for granted; distress arises if she perceives herself as being used.
   - There may be underlying fears of abandonment driving her need to control the relationship dynamics.

4. Potential Negatives of Maternal Protagonism:

1. Emotional Burnout:
- Constantly taking on the nurturing and leading role can lead to emotional exhaustion and burnout, especially if the effort is not reciprocated or appreciated.

2. Imbalance in Relationship Dynamics:
- The relationship may become unbalanced, with one partner consistently in the lead role and the other in a dependent role. This can lead to resentment and a lack of mutual respect.

3. Suppressed Personal Needs:
- The Maternal Protagonist may suppress her own needs and desires to prioritize her partner's, leading to personal dissatisfaction and unfulfilled aspirations.

4. Dependency Issues:
- The partner might become overly dependent on the Maternal Protagonist, hindering their personal growth and ability to take responsibility in the relationship.

5. Conflict and Resentment:
- Over time, the Maternal Protagonist may feel taken for granted or used, leading to conflicts and resentment. This can strain the relationship and potentially lead to its breakdown.

5. Clinical Relevance of Maternal Protagonism

Understanding Relationship Dynamics:
Maternal Protagonism provides valuable insight into the dynamics of caregiving and leadership within relationships.

Recognizing this pattern can help clinicians understand the underlying motivations and behaviors of clients who assume these roles.

Identifying Imbalance and Conflict:
By identifying Maternal Protagonism, therapists can pinpoint potential sources of imbalance and conflict in relationships. This awareness enables them to address issues related to dependency, resentment, and unmet needs, promoting healthier interactions between partners.

Promoting Self-Awareness and Growth:
Understanding Maternal Protagonism allows individuals to gain self-awareness about their caregiving tendencies and leadership roles. Clinicians can guide clients in exploring their motivations and developing strategies to balance their needs with those of their partners.

Supporting Emotional Health:
Therapists can help clients with Maternal Protagonism recognize the signs of emotional burnout and stress associated with their caregiving roles. Interventions can be designed to promote self-care, establish boundaries, and ensure emotional well-being.

Facilitating Mutual Support:
Recognizing Maternal Protagonism in one partner enables clinicians to work with both partners to create mutual support and appreciation. This can lead to more balanced and fulfilling relationships, where both individuals contribute to each other's growth and well-being.

Addressing Childhood Influences:
Understanding the origins of Maternal Protagonism, including childhood experiences and attachment styles, can provide deeper insights into clients' behaviors. Clinicians can work with

clients to address unresolved issues from the past and develop healthier patterns of interaction.

Enhancing Therapeutic Interventions:
Incorporating the concept of Maternal Protagonism into therapeutic interventions can enhance the effectiveness of treatment plans. Clinicians can tailor their approaches to address the specific needs and dynamics associated with this pattern, leading to more successful outcomes.

6. Conclusion:
Maternal Protagonism is a nuanced concept that highlights the interplay between nurturing and leadership in relationships. Recognizing and understanding this behavior can enhance relationship dynamics, ensuring that both partners feel valued and supported.

Source:
Manuel V. Johnson, also known as Ask Dr. Linq, *"Know Thy Man: Learn What Your Man Is Thinking,"* 2024.

APPENDIX F (not a recognized diagnosis)
1. Nurturance Dependency Syndrome

Definition:
Nurturance Dependency Syndrome is a behavioral and psychological condition in which a man actively seeks out relationships with women exhibiting Maternal Protagonism traits. He relies on his partner to provide the necessary guidance, support, and emotional sustenance, as he does not naturally take on a leading or nurturing role within the relationship.

2. Characteristics of Nurturance Dependency Syndrome:

1. Passive in Relationship Dynamics:
- The individual tends to take a backseat in managing both emotional and practical aspects of the relationship.
- Prefers his partner to make decisions and take the lead.

2. Seeking Nurturance:
- Attracted to nurturing and supportive partners who can provide the care and attention he seeks.
- May have a history of being cared for extensively in his family of origin, leading to an expectation of similar treatment in relationships.

3. Avoidance of Responsibility:
- Shies away from taking on significant responsibilities within the relationship.
- Relies on his partner to handle challenging situations and emotional labor.

4. Comfort in Dependence:
- Feels comfortable and secure in a dependent role.
- Finds fulfillment in being cared for and supported.

5. Origins of Behavior:
- This behavior can stem from various psychological and social factors, including childhood experiences and cultural expectations.
- Men who have experienced overprotective or overly nurturing roles in their family of origin may be more likely to exhibit these traits.

6. Impact on Relationships:

- The relationship dynamic can become unbalanced, with one partner consistently in a caretaking role and the other in a dependent role.
- This can lead to resentment and conflict if the nurturer feels taken for granted.

3. Clinical Relevance of Nurturance Dependency Syndrome

Understanding Relationship Dynamics:
Nurturance Dependency Syndrome offers insight into relationship dynamics where one partner consistently assumes a dependent role. Recognizing this pattern helps clinicians understand the underlying motivations and behaviors of clients who rely heavily on their partner for guidance and support.

Identifying Imbalance and Conflict:
By identifying Nurturance Dependency Syndrome, therapists can pinpoint potential sources of imbalance and conflict in relationships. This awareness enables them to address issues related to dependency, lack of initiative, and resentment from the caregiving partner, promoting healthier interactions.

Promoting Self-Awareness and Independence:
Understanding Nurturance Dependency Syndrome allows individuals to gain self-awareness about their dependency tendencies. Clinicians can guide clients in exploring their motivations and developing strategies to increase their independence and self-efficacy within the relationship.

Supporting Emotional Health:
Therapists can help clients recognize the emotional challenges associated with their dependent role, including feelings of insecurity and fear of abandonment. Interventions can be designed

to promote self-care, establish boundaries, and ensure emotional well-being.

Facilitating Mutual Support:
Recognizing Nurturance Dependency Syndrome in one partner enables clinicians to work with both partners to create mutual support and appreciation. This can lead to more balanced and fulfilling relationships, where both individuals contribute to each other's growth and well-being.

Addressing Childhood Influences:
Understanding the origins of Nurturance Dependency Syndrome, including childhood experiences and attachment styles, can provide deeper insights into clients' behaviors. Clinicians can work with clients to address unresolved issues from the past and develop healthier patterns of interaction.

Enhancing Therapeutic Interventions:
Incorporating the concept of Nurturance Dependency Syndrome into therapeutic interventions can enhance the effectiveness of treatment plans. Clinicians can tailor their approaches to address the specific needs and dynamics associated with this pattern, leading to more successful outcomes.

4. Potential Diagnosis:
To diagnose Nurturance Dependency Syndrome, observe the following traits:
- The individual consistently seeks out nurturing and supportive partners.
- Exhibits a passive role in relationship dynamics.
- Avoids significant responsibilities within the relationship.
- Shows comfort and fulfillment in a dependent role.
- Has a history of overprotective or nurturing family dynamics.

5. Conclusion:

Understanding the dynamics of Nurturance Dependency Syndrome is crucial for identifying and addressing relationship imbalances. Recognizing these behaviors can help both partners work towards a more balanced and mutually fulfilling relationship.

Source:
Manuel V. Johnson, also known as Ask Dr. Linq, *"Know Thy Man: Learn What Your Man Is Thinking,"* 2024.

APPENDIX G

The Abundance Mindset and Its Impact on Relationships:

The abundance mindset is a belief that there are plenty of opportunities and resources available in the world. People with this mindset see life as full of possibilities and believe that there is enough success, love, and wealth for everyone. They do not fear scarcity or competition because they trust that they can always find what they need.

In the context of relationships, a person with an abundance mindset believes that there are many potential partners available to them. They feel confident in their ability to attract and connect with others, so they are less likely to become overly attached or desperate in any one relationship. This can lead to a more relaxed and confident attitude, as they do not fear losing one person since they believe they can find another.

This mindset isn't inherently negative but it *can* lead to a man being nonchalant in a relationship because he believes he has many potential partners available to him. This confidence in the availability of other options means he might not feel the need to put in extra effort or show significant concern about any single relationship. Here's how this mindset can contribute to a nonchalant attitude:

1. **Less Investment:** Since he believes he can easily find another partner, he may not invest deeply in the current relationship. This can result in a lack of attentiveness and effort to nurture and maintain the relationship.

2. **Reduced Fear of Loss:** The fear of losing his partner is minimized because he feels confident that he can quickly find someone else. This can make him appear indifferent or unconcerned about the potential end of the relationship.

3. **Lower Emotional Attachment:** With the belief that there are plenty of alternatives, he might not develop a strong emotional attachment to his partner. This can make him seem detached or uninterested.

4. **Casual Approach:** He may adopt a more casual approach to the relationship, avoiding commitment or serious discussions because he doesn't feel a sense of urgency or necessity to secure the relationship.

5. **Lack of Effort:** Believing that he doesn't need to try hard to keep his partner, he may not put in the effort to address issues, show appreciation, or make his partner feel valued. This can lead to a perception of neglect.

428 Know Thy Man

APPENDIX H
Biological Influences

1. Differences in Brain Structure
- **Source:** Cahill, L. (2006). "Why sex matters for neuro-science". *Nature Reviews Neuroscience*, 7(6), 477-484.
- **Summary:** This review discusses the structural and functional differences between male and female brains, highlighting how these differences influence behavior and cognition.
- **Citation:** Cahill, L. (2006). Why sex matters for neuroscience. *Nature Reviews Neuroscience,* 7(6), 477-484. https://doi.org/10.1038/nrn1909

2. Emotional Processing and Decision-Making
- **Source:** Gur, R. C., & Gur, R. E. (2016). "Sex differences in brain and behavior: Hormones versus genes". **Brain Research**, 1645, 190-197.
- **Summary:** This study explores how hormonal and genetic differences between males and females influence emotional processing and decision-making.
- **Citation:** Gur, R. C., & Gur, R. E. (2016). Sex differences in brain and behavior: Hormones versus genes. *Brain Research,* 1645, 190-197. https://doi.org/10.1016/j.brainres.2016.03.037

Evolutionary Psychology

3. Evolutionary Traits and Behavior
- **Source:** Buss, D. M. (1995). "Evolutionary psychology: A new paradigm for psychological science". *Psychological Inquiry*, 6(1), 1-30.
- **Summary:** This foundational paper by David Buss outlines the principles of evolutionary psychology and

explains how evolutionary pressures have shaped human behavior, including male traits such as competitiveness and risk-taking.

- **Citation:** Buss, D. M. (1995). Evolutionary psychology: A new paradigm for psychological science. *Psychological Inquiry*, 6(1), 1-30. https://doi.org/10.1207/s15327965pli0601_1

4. Sexual Selection and Human Behavior

- **Source:** Miller, G. F. (2000). "Sexual selection for indicators of intelligence". *The Mating Mind: How Sexual Choice Shaped the Evolution of Human Nature*. New York: Doubleday.
- **Summary:** Geoffrey Miller's book discusses how sexual selection has driven the evolution of human traits, including intelligence and social behaviors, which are particularly relevant to understanding male behavior.
- **Citation:** Miller, G. F. (2000). Sexual selection for indicators of intelligence. In *The Mating Mind: How Sexual Choice Shaped the Evolution of Human Nature*. New York: Doubleday.

Societal Expectations and Conditioning

5. Impact of Societal Norms

- **Source:** Courtenay, W. H. (2000). "Constructions of masculinity and their influence on men's well-being: A theory of gender and health". *Social Science & Medicine*, 50(10), 1385-1401.
- **Summary:** This article examines how societal constructions of masculinity affect men's health behaviors and well-being, providing insight into how societal norms influence male behavior.

- **Citation:** Courtenay, W. H. (2000). Constructions of masculinity and their influence on men's well-being: A theory of gender and health. *Social Science & Medicine*, 50(10), 1385-1401. https://doi.org/10.1016/S0277-9536(99)00390-1

6. Cultural Influences on Masculinity
- **Source:** Connell, R. W. (2005). *Masculinities* (2nd ed.). Berkeley: University of California Press.
- **Summary:** R.W. Connell's seminal work explores the concept of masculinity and its variations across different cultures, providing a comprehensive analysis of how cultural expectations shape male behavior.

Citation: Connell, R. W. (2005). *Masculinities* (2nd ed.). Berkeley: University of California Press.

KNOW
THY
MAN

GRATITUDE

Writing a book is a journey that cannot be undertaken alone. I owe a deep debt of gratitude to many who have made this particular book possible.

My heartfelt thanks go to my mother, Trudy. Your inspiring words kept me steady when I slipped and lost my way. Your unwavering support and belief in my potential have been the foundation of my journey. You've always wished for me to achieve wonderful things in life and have often been my biggest cheerleader. Thank you.

To my father, Manuel, thank you for passing on your critical thinking, leadership mentality, and height (lol). Your genetic gifts have profoundly shaped the man I am today. Your ability to turn adversity into opportunity is truly inspiring. Thank you.

To my son, Mareion, my life's motivation, you are the reason I strive for greatness. As you reach adulthood, I hope to be a shining example for you and will always be here to help you navigate life's challenges. Know that I will always speak to you with your best interests at heart. I'm grateful to have you in my life every day.

To my stepfather, Dana, you have been a remarkable example of what a man should be for his family. Your guidance and teachings have greatly influenced my journey. Your support in my life is unparalleled. Thank you.

To my mentor, Sol Davis, thank you for your invaluable guidance in shaping my business mindset. Your lessons on management, engagement, poise, and the value of hard work have been instrumental in my success. Thank you.

To my close friend, Aicha, who recognized my dormant potential and motivated me to continue this book. Without your encouragement that night, Aicha, I'm not sure this mission would have been completed. Thank you for your trust in me; it is why I trust in myself.

To the women I have interacted with throughout my life, you have been my inspiration and my teachers, often without realizing it. I would not be where I am today without you. For the dark times in my life, the many mistakes I've made, I thank you for the corrective wisdom you've shared.

I am incredibly grateful to all my enthusiastic readers and followers across all my Ask Dr. Linq platforms. Your words, emails, questions, comments, and video shares are the motivation that keeps me going and kept me writing. I am deeply thankful for all of you, especially the thousands of women who have reached out with their relationship challenges. I hope this book can be your guide.

To all the men I've spoken with upon taking on this task, I thank you for your insight into worlds I could have never visited without your guidance. Thank you.

To my immediate and extended family, my cousins, aunts, and uncles, I love you all. Thank you.

Last but certainly not least, I give my deepest, most humble thanks and gratitude to my personal Lord and Savior, Jesus Christ (**ישוע**). Our relationship has kept me focused on finishing this book for your children. Thank you for allowing me to share these words with the world and for being patient with me when I was not allowing you to lead the way.

Thank you all for your support and for being a part of this incredible journey.
I love you.

Manuel V. Johnson

IN MEMORY OF

WHITNEY NICOLE

November 28, 1986 – September 8, 2024

Dear friend, the book you encouraged me to write is
finally complete. I know you'll be reading from up
above. Just tell God I apologize for the swear words.
There wouldn't be an Ask Dr. Linq without you.
Your inspiring words and infectious smile will be
missed. I thank you for sharing this life with me.
Until we meet again…
Love you and may you rest in peace.

1 Peter 3:8-9 (NLT):

FINALLY, ALL OF YOU SHOULD BE OF ONE MIND. SYMPATHIZE WITH EACH OTHER. LOVE EACH OTHER AS BROTHERS AND SISTERS. BE TENDERHEARTED, AND KEEP A HUMBLE ATTITUDE. DON'T REPAY EVIL FOR EVIL. DON'T RETALIATE WITH INSULTS WHEN PEOPLE INSULT YOU. INSTEAD, PAY THEM BACK WITH A BLESSING. THAT IS WHAT GOD HAS CALLED YOU TO DO, AND HE WILL GRANT YOU HIS BLESSING.

MAY CHRIST BLESS YOU ON YOUR NEW JOURNEY

Made in United States
Troutdale, OR
05/06/2025

31147743R00256